1000 Days to the Bar
But the Practice of Law
Begins Now

Dennis J. Tonsing

William S. Hein & Co., Inc.
Buffalo, New York
2003

Library of Congress Cataloging-in-Publication Data

Tonsing, Dennis J.
　1000 days to the bar—but the practice of law begins now /
Dennis J. Tonsing.

　　p.cm.
　Includes bibliographical references.
　ISBN 0-8377-3726-5 (paper : alk. paper)
　1. Law—Study and teaching—United States. 2. Practice of
law—United States. I. Title: One thousand days to the bar—
but the practice of law begins now. II. Title.
KF272.T66 2003
340.'071'173　　　　　　　　　　　　　　　2003056610

2nd printing 2004

Printed in the United States of America

This volume is printed on acid-free paper.

Dedication

To the two women who have given me life,
Mary Ellen and Kristy.

To the two men who added life to my practice of law,
Jon and Richard.

CONTENTS

ACKNOWLEDGMENTS

Since my first days at Southwestern University School of Law in 1970, I have been fascinated with the relationship between the study of law and the practice of law. At Southwestern, I learned from many educators who had practiced law for many years. They brought the wisdom, the spirit, and the professional dignity of practitioners into the classroom every day, and instilled a liveliness into my education that made law school a fascinating and wonderful experience for me. Under the wings of Professors Karlin, Hirschberg, Rocca, Mennell, Goodman, and others, I learned that to do well in law school, one must *practice* law.

It was Ruta Stropus, Assistant Dean for Educational Services at DePaul University College of Law, who encouraged me to enter the field of law school academic support; again, it was Dean Stropus and her co-author, Charlotte Taylor, DePaul's Assistant Dean for Multicultural Affairs, who—by the publication of their own superb book on academic success—encouraged me to publish.

What I have learned about academic support I have learned from three sources:

- My colleagues who have dedicated themselves to helping students navigate through law schools across the country—the academic support professionals. Too numerous to mention individually, they are the women and men who attend the annual national and regional conferences sponsored by the Law School Admission Council and the annual Association of American Law Schools conferences. They confer, they write, they publish, they constantly communicate via e-mail and telephone—they help each other and they help law students become lawyers.
- Those educators with whom I have worked at Vermont Law School and Roger Williams University School of Law, who have continually encouraged me to innovate.
- The hundreds of law students who have attended my presentations in law schools and at CLEO conferences, worked with me one-to-one, sat through my doctrinal classes, worked with me as mentors, and always—intentionally or not—provided me with feedback.

Informed readers may hear echoes of the voice of Professor Vernellia Randall as they sift through the "nuts and bolts" sections of this book. Through her speaking and writing she has not only taught me, she has also inspired countless academic support professionals, law students, and ultimately, practicing lawyers across the country. Many of the ideas you will read in this book are sprouts from seeds planted by my sources of learning. I have done my best to attribute those ideas to their generators. To all of these mentors, teachers, students, colleagues and friends I say "Thank you."

Several friends have reviewed various versions of the manuscript as it developed and contributed thoughtful comments and suggestions. For this I thank Dean David Logan, Professors Pavel Wonsowicz and Anne Lawton and law student Marta Garrett. During her last year of law school, Rebecca Smith assisted greatly with cite-checking and reviewing quotations for accuracy. For administrative support during the final phases of writing, I thank Tracy Sartrys; for invaluable assistance in rounding up books to summarize, I tip my hat to Cynthia Spencer and Marianne Couture. Thank you to Writing Specialist Kim Baker for many hours of painstaking proofreading and editing, and to Kristy Tonsing for proofreading and for providing many motivational moments.

Three years ago, Sheila Jarrett, Publications Manager for William S. Hein & Co., Inc., encouraged me to write this book. Even as the book went to press, she continued to support me. Sheila recognized the importance of the message in this book, and followed through. For this I am grateful.

FOREWORD

"Such is the unity of history," Frederick Pollock and Frederic Maitland began their classic history of English law, "that anyone who endeavors to tell a piece of it must feel that his first sentence tears at a seamless web." In the ensuing century, generations of legal thinkers have debated whether, in fact, all legal principles within a culture are tied, at some basic level, to all other principles, no matter how far removed on the surface. Suffice it to say, this fundamental question remains open for debate, perhaps for the ages.

Dennis Tonsing, however, in his book *1000 Days to the Bar—But the Practice of Law Begins Now*, proceeds on a deep intuition about the practice of law that is similar to the notion of the "seamless web"—that the successful practice of law involves the sum total of dozens of smaller skills, and that the first day of law school is not merely the next day of school, but rather the first day of practice. This understanding of the link between legal education and the real world of law practice is not new; the American Bar Association's influential McCrate Report (1992) emphasized the need for legal education to better prepare law students to be practicing lawyers. However, the Report's many recommendations were directed at changing the behavior of law *schools*. Dean Tonsing's focus is on law *students*, and his goal—showing law students how every one of their activities, even those that appear to be drudgery, is a direct predecessor of, and an essential aspect of a skill used by practicing lawyers—results in a refreshing clarity about the link between the immediate and the permanent.

1000 Days does more than point out the link; it shows how a law student's daily activities promote accomplishment of what are every student's three goals:

- developing a rich, deep understanding of legal principles necessary to the successful practice of law;
- earning grades that reflect each student's personal best effort; and
- passing the bar exam on the first try.

Dean Tonsing identifies core aspects of a law student's responsibilities and unfailingly helps the reader appreciate his/her link to the practice of law. Foremost, he emphasizes "active learning," cognizant that the student who attends class as a scrivener is not likely the student who best understands and can use the legal principles developed by the professor. He recognizes that a student's tuition dollars are, at base, paying for a student to be quizzed by a professor; as a result, every student should consider every question asked of any student to be one directed at him or her, maximizing the intellectual moment. He then explains why such active listening is essential to successful practice, whether it is in the service of an advocate who listens closely to the direct examination in an effort to craft an effective cross-examination based upon what the witness actually says, or the transactional lawyer who hopes to tailor her pitch to the specific, articulated needs of the client.

Similarly, Dean Tonsing emphasizes the practical nature of learning the law, and that knowledge of legal principles and policies are useless unless the student (and later the practicing lawyer) can use them to solve problems. This means that law students must constantly check to see that they can use what they know (I often tell first-year law students that I don't grade them on what they *know* in their head but rather what they *show* on the paper) in the context of solving the concrete legal problems presented on the exam. This is just as true for the practicing lawyer, whose client wants help solving an actual legal problem and cares not a whit for whether the lawyer knows "the law."

1000 Days provides great value by pointing out these links, but it doesn't stop there. It provides hundreds of practical tips to help law students make every day in law school a small, but essential step, in the direction of the successful practice of law. Some of my favorites include:

- how to prepare for class;
- how to take notes effectively;
- how to identify key concepts by picking up on cues provided by teachers;
- how to synthesize briefs and class notes in order to compose an effective course outline;
- how to create and use flow charts;
- how to internalize (as opposed to memorize) course material;
- how to make every day a preparation for law school exams;
- how to begin preparing for the bar exam;
- how to manage scarce time.

All of this valuable material is presented in Dean Tonsing's crisp, readable style. I especially enjoyed the material presented in boxes in the margin—like footnotes, but more fun—that trace the linguistic roots of many terms ("dog-eared" means that the corners of a well-thumbed book resemble the "floppy ears of a dog"), or the occasional wry observation (as when he quotes Abraham Lincoln, "A lawyer's time is his stock in trade," and then observes, "Apparently our sixteenth president knew no female attorneys ... not unusual in the nineteenth century.").

In sum, *1000 Days* is a very valuable resource for law students, both because of its foundational concept—that the first day of law school and every day thereafter is inherently part of the practice of law—and the practical suggestions that, if followed, will enable novice lawyers to achieve their goals.

David A. Logan
Dean
Roger Williams University
Ralph R. Papitto School of Law

PREFACE

This book has but one objective: empowerment. Most law students have been anticipating the start of law school for weeks, months or years —some for a lifetime. They approach the start of school with a mix of excitement and apprehension, often with a sense of awe at the majesty of the enterprise they are about to begin. This hopeful group includes a mightily gifted, dynamic, achievement-oriented variety of individuals. They are determined to do well—and they should be. They have been selected by admissions committees across America adept at selecting only those students with the capability to succeed in law school, pass the bar examination, and enter into the professional practice of law.

Why, then, do so many first-year law students express high levels of anxiety, depression, isolation, "drowning," a sense of imminent and inevitable failure, intense frustration, lack of control, and ominous foreboding within 90 days of beginning school?

There are reasons. Most have recently exited successful positions of academic, social or executive leadership. They believe the institution they are entering—a "school"—is merely an advanced version of what they were so good at before—"school." This belief is well founded, for the institution they are about to attend is called a "school," and each matriculant has just completed these familiar "school" tasks:

- Application process, including writing an essay about goals.
- Purchase of a stack of expensive, important-looking, heavy books.
- Attendance at orientation.
- Campus tour—walking through school building hallways filled with pictures of former students in caps and gowns, passing offices of an assortment of deans, professors and identifiable administrators (Registrar, loan counselors and librarians).

No wonder they believe they are back for another semester of "school." That's even what the sign on the front of the building tells them. But they are not in school. They have just entered the practice of law—complete with everything except the clients and the paychecks.

Law students who approach law school, day after day, as if they are "students" going to "school" become confused and suffer the problems mentioned above. Law students who realize that the first day of law school is the first day of their career as lawyers are the law students who are ready to be empowered. They know they are about to begin to

> In the fall of 2001, only 53 percent of the 90,900 students who applied to ABA-approved law schools were enrolled (based on Law School Admission Council statistics).

> Are these feelings inevitable? Are they a necessary part of the development from law student to lawyer? The answer to both questions is clear: "No."

> "Law students," one writer glibly observes, "are almost always anxious and afraid." James E. Moliterno & Fredric I. Lederer, *An Introduction to Law, Law Study, and the Lawyer's Role* 160 (Carolina Academic Press, 1991).

practice law; they need instruction in *how* to practice law. This book provides that instruction.

An underlying premise of this book is that as law students commence their studies, they intend to do their personal best on the path to their doctoral degree and throughout their professional career. Thus, the thrust of this book is toward that goal—excellence. That lofty but ambiguous goal is more easily approached if it is divided into its most immediately realizable components:

> You should have realized by now that this is not a "survival guide" to law school. If your approach to law school is based on the mindset that you are in for 1000 days of torture, that you will be lucky to pass your first round of exams, and that those who earn their doctoral degrees are mere "survivors," you should return this book to the bookstore, or sell it to a friend—or commit to drastically modifying your frame of mind.

- A rich, deep foundation for the professional practice of law.
- Grades reflecting the student's personal best effort.
- First-time bar passage.

No one would suggest that to graduate from law school, to eventually pass a bar exam, or to practice law, everyone needs to follow the program set out in this book. Frankly, most students can achieve *those* simple objectives with a minimum of time and effort. If you are reading these words, thinking, "All I want to do is graduate—that's enough for me," then you probably ought to skim the pages, just to get the sense of what others around you are doing. On the other hand, if you are thinking, "I want to work at my highest levels for these next 1000 days, while enjoying academic success, a satisfying family and social life, and fully preparing for an exciting and rewarding career as a lawyer," read on carefully.

Ninety-Day Trial Recommendation

After you have read a significant part of this book, you may say to yourself, "The rigor, detail, time commitment and strategizing that this book suggests is wholly unnecessary—I'll do just fine by simply studying harder than I did in college—much harder." Reconsider. Law school is not like college. Law school is your opportunity to begin the practice of law.

You have 1000 days until you sit for the bar examination—but you have only 90 days until you sit for your first semester final examinations. Consider following all the suggestions in this book for 90 days. Ninety days. That's all. I suggest you take to heart the lessons presented here, and accept my challenge to commit to the practice of law in law school with the same rigor, detail, planning and strategizing that you intend to employ in the professional practice of law. Take your finals with confidence and self-assurance. Note your grade point average. Then determine whether it was worth it.

PART ONE

THE PRACTICE OF LAW BEGINS
ON THE FIRST DAY OF LAW SCHOOL

Shifting the Paradigm

The *American Heritage Dictionary* defines "practice" as the "exercise of an occupation or a profession." That's the way the term is used in the acclaimed weekly television drama of the same name. Once a lawyer passes a licensing examination, she is allowed to enter "the practice." Before a lawyer is allowed to enter "the practice," she must leap over significant hurdles: six semesters of law school—including at least a dozen final examinations and a bar examination. Some see this series of tests as obstacles, impediments, obstructions on the road to "the practice." I see them as essential learning opportunities. I see them as the practice.

Consider this alternate *American Heritage Dictionary* definition of practice: "Repeated performance of an activity in order to learn or perfect a skill." Law students certainly learn laws—rules pertaining to justice, and the orderly administration of social and governmental affairs. They learn constitutional principles. They learn the intricacies of the legal system. But every law professor will tell you that "you are not here to learn a string of rules, of elements, of 'black letter law.' Rather," they will insist, "you are at law school to learn how to think and write like a lawyer."

They are right. Ideally, the law school experience will help you become a lawyer, not simply a person who has learned lots of laws. The difference is immense. Anyone who can memorize can learn the law. If it were that simple, the LSAT would test hopeful students' aptitudes for memorizing. But it doesn't—instead, it tests aptitude for analysis. In order to succeed in law school, a student needs to employ the highest levels of reasoning; in order to excel in law school, a student must manifest expertise in the highest levels of *legal* reasoning.

An excellent law student becomes a lawyer. The "becoming" is a gradual process, a growth in many directions on many paths. The student who spends three years learning laws—following only a few of these paths—is destined to spend more years after law school, engaged in the "repeated performance of an activity in order to learn or perfect a skill." Why not learn the "skill" of lawyering during law school? That is, begin the practice now.

Law school provides students with the essential training ground to repeatedly perform the activities lawyers engage in daily. What do lawyers do daily? Which of these activities do you recognize as functions you envision yourself performing as you practice law professionally?

- Fluently speaking, reading, writing, and comprehending the language of the law.
- Persuading others through language use.

> "Law students do not suddenly become lawyers at some magical point; rather, they spend all of their time in law school *becoming*." Molitemo & Lederer, 174.

> "To become an outstanding lawyer," Stetson Law School's Dean Emeritus, Bruce R. Jacob writes, "one must be courageous, independent-minded, honest, conscientious, and ethical. These traits should be nurtured and further developed while in law school. Concurrently, new abilities and skills should be acquired. The student learns to self-teach and to be self-critical." Bruce R. Jacob, *Developing Lawyering Skills and The Nurturing of Inherent Traits and Abilities*, 29 Stetson L. Rev. 1057, 1073 (2000).

- Continually self-evaluating performance and making needed corrections.
- Recognizing legal issues where non-lawyers do not.
- Prioritizing objectives and the multiple tasks designed to achieve them.
- Strategically planning to accomplish well-defined objectives.
- Using time efficiently and effectively.
- Asking questions calculated to inform.
- Exercising as much control over the use of each day and week as events and circumstances allow.
- Organizing—and reorganizing—to achieve specific (sometimes shifting) goals.
- Managing time advantageously, expecting the unexpected.
- Operating within groups—as participants or leaders.
- Recognizing the need to work within a rigidly structured—sometimes antagonistic—organizational framework, to achieve self-defined objectives.
- Self-directing, self-motivating, self-propelling.
- Learning (and relearning) alone—without an instructor.
- Remembering vast quantities of material.
- Digesting and writing volumes—letters, pleadings, appeals, briefs, memoranda, contracts, leases, opinions, analyses.
- Engaging in dialectic (the exercise of arriving at the truth by the exchange of logical arguments).
- Exercising self-control.
- Briefing cases and statutes.
- Remaining calm while operating under stressful conditions.
- Maintaining composure while peers are exhibiting anxiety.
- Carefully balancing the practice of law with family, social, and physical needs and obligations.

Orville and Wilbur Wright did not arrive at Kitty Hawk one day and fly the next. Their longer and longer glides, then powered flights, grew "out of an aptitude for learning how to do a difficult thing. It was a simple method but rare. They broke a job into its parts and proceeded one part at a time. They practiced each small task until they mastered it, then moved on....Wilbur said, 'skill comes by the constant repetition....'" James Tobin, *To Fly!* 34 Smithsonian 50, 56 (April 2003).

Although many law students view law school as a series of classes—in which they are taught laws, maxims, elements, definitions, jurisprudential theories, policy considerations—I find this view to be disturbingly narrow and myopic. The lessons of law school are geared to teach lawyers how to practice law. "To learn to play the flute," Aristotle claimed, "you must play the flute." To learn to practice law, you must practice law—and practicing law means *actively* engaging in the activities listed above. I maintain that the law student who consciously, conscientiously, and vigorously practices law for 1000 days—as described throughout this book—will reach the highest academic level she is capable of attaining in law school, will be extraordinarily prepared to enter into the final phases of bar examination preparedness, and will leap across the bar and into the professional practice with dynamism and confidence.

The time span between your first day of law school and the bar examination is about 1000 days—you can spend this 1000-day period waiting, thinking of yourself as a deskbound schoolchild, or you can begin practicing law and continue for 1000 days. I suggest the latter.

Start practicing law today. You have 1000 days to practice—then it's for real.

Law School Is Not School

Professors, academic support personnel, experienced students—all will advise you about the relationship between your undergraduate experience and the law school experience. The advice they provide is often helpful but misleading in one essential respect. Here's why: elementary school is school. High school is school. College is school. Law school is *not* school. The relationship between your undergraduate academic experience and the adventure of law school is not one best expressed by any comparison between the two. Law school is so different from your undergraduate experience because it is not (at all) "school" as the word is commonly used.

Note the passive use of the verb "to educate." You will quickly note the distinction in law school—passive versus active learning.

A school is an establishment wherein students are educated. Those who instruct within a school do the educating—these "educators" are referred to as "teachers." Teachers teach—that is, they impart knowledge. Certainly, law professors impart knowledge. However, this impartation is only a by-product of their more profound objectives—the chief endeavors of law professors relate more to discourse, dialectic, discussion and analytical exercise—most law professors attend class to engage students in discussion, the point of which is to stimulate learning, to deepen and enrich the experience of learning the law. But the chore of "teaching," as you know it—the imparting of knowledge by an educator—is not borne by the law professor. That is now *your* job. School is over. The years of being taught have concluded. Lawyers self-educate. Welcome to the practice.

Modern law professors expect students to actively engage them, the subject matter, and each other—challenging, reaffirming, and developing. Professor Laurie Morin, from the University of the District of Columbia's School of Law explains:

> *The task of the teacher is to provide a learning space that bounds the inquiry with appropriate texts or source material, while leaving room for the students to look inward and engage with one another and the materials from the perspective of their own experience, beliefs, and insights—to test their beliefs and values against the norms of the profession and against one another.*[1]

Thus, discussions centered on the similarities and differences between law school and undergraduate education are largely irrelevant. Undergraduate education is for "under" graduates ... you are well beyond that. Certainly, many of the skills you developed during your scholastic life will prove valuable in the practice of law, just as many of the skills you learned that made you a better bicycle rider proved valuable when you became an automobile driver, or just as many of the skills you learned as a Girl Scout proved valuable when you became a Marine. However, because the endeavors are on such different levels, *comparison* is inapposite—Ferraris are not Schwinns; the Marine Corps is no Girl Scout troop.

Describing law school in collegiate terms confuses law students. Describing law school in career terms enlightens students. When a college graduate is admitted to law school, we say she "matriculates"—the stem of this word is "matrix." In law school, students who actively engage in their surroundings originate and develop the knowledge base, the skill sets, and the cognitive strategies essential to success in their careers—careers that extend from law school orientation through retirement from the active practice of law. On the other hand, students who passively attend "school" are less likely to achieve these goals (origination and development) with the speed and depth of those who avidly begin their careers on day one of the law school experience.

> A "matrix" is a situation or surrounding substance within which something else originates or develops.

During your first year of law school you will discover that you have quite a bit of work to do. A first-year law school course load (about 15 credits each semester), usually includes Torts, Contracts, Civil Procedure, Legal Research and Writing, and often Property, Constitutional Law, and Criminal Law. In this context, "I'm drowning," is a frequent complaint among first-semester law students. "All I want to do is keep my head above water—I feel completely overwhelmed." These aquatic metaphors are apt. Often, law students find themselves awash in a flood of uncategorized information—facts and theories disconnected from, alien to, often at odds with their intuition, their preconceived ideas, their personal experiences. As the flood continues, the churning waters begin to soak the students and to drag them down. Just as hopeless drowning swimmers succumb to the raging surf and surrender control to this puissant force of nature, so also do too many wunnelles capitulate to the perceived inevitability of loss of control. This is the passive reaction. This is the reaction that keeps law students from achieving their "personal bests" during their first semester. They've heard it's hard, they encounter the proof of the difficulty of law school during the first three weeks—they feel "overwhelmed."

> To "whelm" is to submerge, to cover over with water.

> Legal educators often refer to first-year law students as "1L's"—pronounced, "wunnelles."

Avoid this. Be proactive. Proactive means acting in advance to deal with an anticipated difficulty. You know law school will provide difficulties. Set up your systematic program to deal with the difficulties before they engulf you like a raging tsunami. How? From the first day of law school be in control. Begin the practice by employing the executive-function tools lawyers employ.

> However, as the Honorable John C. Thomas put it at the Marshall-Wythe School of Law, "[I]f you truly learn how to swim you will not care whether the water is 10 feet deep or 10,000 feet deep … because you will be swimming on the top." Moliterno & Lederer, 6.

Law school success is largely a matter of self-control. The more you exercise strong control over your life, your curriculum, your extra-curricular activities and your health, the more you increase the probability of hitting your mark. The more you surrender control to others and to circumstances, the more you increase the probability of falling short of your mark.

Here's an example: are you about to let a professor's unpleasant personality, ambiguity, undesirable teaching style, pedantry, or severity adversely affect your career? In law schools across the country, these explanations are offered daily for lack of preparation, classroom truancy, refusal to brief cases, and (finally) poor exam performance:

- I can't stand the professor.
- She doesn't lay out the law for us.
- He doesn't make the subject interesting.
- She tells us to read six cases, and then only talks about one during class.
- He intimidates me.

"Competence as a law student is nearly as demanding as competence as a lawyer. It demands that the student take personal responsibility for his or her legal education. It is not enough to say, 'The professor didn't cover it;' if you need to learn it, *learn it* even if you research it yourself. If the professor seems to be in error, question the statement." Moliterno & Lederer, 175.

Are the students who offer these explanations the ones who will one day explain courtroom losses to their clients by telling them, "I can't stand the judge"? Are these the students who will explain their failure to include a necessary item in a lease by informing their clients that the lease just wasn't very interesting? And will they someday tell their clients that the negotiations worked out unfavorably because the mediator intimidated them?

The time to practice proactivity is while you attend law school. Ideally, you will be an expert at it (at a doctoral level) when you are admitted to the bar.

Grades Are By-Products

A by-product is a side effect, that is, something produced during the process of making something else. Focusing on grades is unnecessary. Quality grades will be produced as you engage in the process of making yourself an excellent lawyer. "Quality grades" are grades reflecting your personal best. Because of differing capabilities, different levels of interest, diverse scholastic goals, disparate career expectations, and grading curves, not all students will achieve extraordinarily high grade-point averages. However, each student should achieve the GPA she sets her sight on.

If law schools are doing their jobs well, it stands to reason that their measurement techniques—tools by which individual professors assess whether and to what extent the individual students assigned to their classes have succeeded in attaining the objectives announced by the professor—are valid and at least moderately accurate. Thus, first-rate preparation aimed at superlative performance on each course's final examination should satisfy two parallel student objectives:

- The objective of achieving grades accurately reflecting the level of learning.
- The objective of laying a solid foundation for the professional practice of law.

Therefore, while focusing on grades is unnecessary (and very often counter-productive), focusing on appearing for your final examinations with a complete array of skills, knowledge, adaptability, and self-confidence is essential. Proper exam-targeted study, as defined within this book, is the highest yielding way to study law in law school. Exam-targeted study is "practicing law."

> Whether law schools are doing a fine job of educating lawyers is a matter of opinion—and there are as many opinions as there are lawyers, law professors, and law school deans. Exhaustive apologias on the subject abound in legal education journals—but focusing on that debate during the first year of law school is unproductive. You have entered the system—thrive in it.

Lawyers Work Long Hours

An insidious effect of the tendency to think of law school as "school," instead of as the practice of law, relates to the amount of time one spends in the active pursuit of her objectives. Unfortunately, college is not all that difficult for many bright students. How many college students attend every class and study two or more hours outside of class for every hour in the classroom? Did you? Thinking that law school is but one large step up from undergraduate school, many students fall way behind in the first 60 days of school—they can't figure out what's happening. After all, they are studying twice as many hours as they did at UCLA or Rutgers or Howard or Notre Dame—but they are still very confused. They put in twice the time (say, 25 hours outside of class), use the same study methods, and feel lost. The problem is clear—these students entered law school believing they were still in *school*. They assumed that their professors would teach them and that they would learn as they always did—by reading quickly and thoroughly, by taking copious notes in class, and by reviewing their books and notes. These students fail to grasp that school is over—they fail to understand that they have entered into the practice of law. During college, they learned what students do to achieve their goals—and they did it well; now they need to learn what *lawyers* do to achieve their goals.

Ask recently employed law graduates to describe their work weeks, and you will find that a schedule such as this is typical (or lighter than usual): full days (for example, 7:30 to 5:30 with a half-hour lunch), a couple evenings (for example, 6:00 to 10:00), and a half day on the weekend (for example, 8:00 to 12:30 on Saturday). That's 60 hours each week.[2] Of course, the workload varies from week to week, from firm to firm, and from lawyer to lawyer.

If you intend to practice law from the outset of law school, plan to devote similar quantities of time to your career, starting with the first week of that career—the first week of law school. A class load of 15 credits usually equates to about 15 hours in the classroom—that leaves 45 hours for the rest of your practice, if you are working 60 hours a week at your career. For some, this will be enough time—others may need more or less. But the first-year law student who spends *substantially* less time is not taking advantage of what these three years have to offer and is less likely to perform at her personal best level.

That's *why* to study and how much to study ... but *what* do you study and *how* do you do it? Read on.

"Law school," Professors Stropus and Taylor advise, "requires 100% of your time." Ruta K. Stropus & Charlotte D. Taylor, *Bridging the Gap Between College and Law School* 138 (Carolina Academic Press, 2001). You should count on spending at least as much time practicing law in law school as you intend to spend during the remainder of your career, in the professional practice.

Lawyers Are Fluent in the Language of the Law

Language is medium, process and product in the various arenas of the law where legal texts, spoken or written, are generated in the service of regulating social behavior. Particularly in literate cultures, once norms and proceedings are recorded, standardized and institutionalized, a special legal language develops, representing a predictable process and pattern of functional specialization. In the Anglo-Saxon common law system, a discrete legal language has been apparent since post-Conquest England, which in many essentials has persisted to the present day.[3]

The "discrete legal language" referred to above is the language of the law. Those who speak and write this "special" language are members of a "speech community"—a term linguists use to define a group of people who share a language, a dialect, or a "variety" of a language. Fluency in the language of the law is a prerequisite for admission to, and full acceptance and participation in, the legal community. For better or worse, the sharing of this common language promotes cohesiveness within the culture of the law and enables "in-group" members to sort out the world in the same or complementary ways—maintaining "cognitive solidarity" within the professional community.[4]

> No one can demonstrate extraordinary proficiency in any field of knowledge, without being able to speak the language spoken by the practitioners within that field.

> Some would argue—with substantial merit—the "common language" promotes *exclusion*.

Modern law firms ... expect new associates to make conclusions based on sound analysis and to communicate those conclusions both orally and in writing in a comprehensive and intelligent fashion.[5]

Indeed, one of the aims of bar examiners is to test your fluency[6]—to determine whether you will be admitted to their community. What is this "fluency"? One who speaks and writes "fluently" (read "flowingly") is one who is able to engage in oral and written discourse intelligibly without apparent effort.

> The root of the word "fluency" is the Latin verb *fluere*, "to flow."

Since professors and bar examiners nationwide proclaim that they want to see evidence that examinees are able to write "like lawyers," rapid and continuous development of fluency in the language of the law would seem to be an obvious essential element in the education of a novice lawyer. Writing in this "special" language means far more than simply writing with due regard for the law's specialized jargon and characteristic syntax. The writing must also be "intelligible"—intelligibility to the legal community means apprehensible to lawyers and jurists, cogent, intellectually tight. Because the nature and purposes of legal

The careful and persuasive aspects of the language of lawyers have been described by Anthony Amsterdam (Professor at NYU School of Law) and Jerome Bruner (NYU Professor of cultural psychology) thusly: "Rhetorics enable lawyers in the service of their clients . . . to justify their categorizations and to tell their stories in a language that navigates adroitly between certifiable misrepresentation and acknowledgement of the weakness of their client's positions.... It is a subtle discourse, full of implications that it insulates from the risk of refutation by stopping millimeters short of assertion, and from the risk of backfire by embroidering with equivocations at the margins of commitment." Anthony G. Amsterdam & Jerome Bruner, *Minding the Law* 14 (Harvard University Press, 2000).

This is a question for which the expression "duh" was coined.

discourse require precision and lucidity, intelligibility in legal speaking and writing is also marked by clarity, accuracy, appropriate use of conventional technical legal language, and attention to semantic details and distinctions. To fulfill these intellect-oriented criteria, the author of the writing must be able to think as lawyers think. In order to think as lawyers think, one must speak and write as lawyers speak and write; language fluency and thoughts conceived in that language are inextricably intertwined.

Fluency in the language of the law and "thinking like a lawyer" are so intricately interwoven that simultaneous development of both should be a goal of every serious law student. Both are readily apparent to professors, bar examiners, literate lawyers, and jurists alike—as is the absence of either. Legal jargon is lost without the emblematic matrix of legal reasoning to support it; legal analysis can't be appropriately communicated without an abundant legal vocabulary used with precision, grace and cogency. Perhaps more importantly, legal analysis can't take place without the dynamic mental machinery and intellectual horsepower included in fluency in the language of the law.

As a practical matter, since professors can't actually see what students are thinking, they do the next best thing to determine if students are thinking as lawyers think. That is, they scrutinize the product of that thought—student answers to examination questions. Thus, *exam answers provide professors with measurable evidence of whether, and to what extent, their students are thinking like lawyers think.* Students who earn high grades in courses dependent upon writings as evaluative instruments, demonstrate fluency in the language of the law.

Consider this—the professor is the one who will assign a grade to your exam answer; don't you increase the likelihood of achieving a higher grade if you provide essay responses to exam questions written fluently in the language of the professor?

Achieving Fluency in the Language of the Law

Have you learned a foreign language? Are you fluent? Most who have achieved fluency in a non-native language recognize that their learning could be divided into four major categories:

- Input—what goes in.
- Internalization—what sticks inside and is used to produce the output.
- Output—what comes out.
- Feedback—verification of accuracy, or highlighting of inaccuracy, essential for correction.

Foreign language input occurs through the learner's listening and reading. The internalization includes memorizing and organizing—establishing and understanding meanings of, and relationships between, foreign words and phrases. The output takes place when the learner speaks and writes. The feedback is offered by oral and written conversational participants—either by direct compliment or correction or by nonverbal activity consistent with the communicative objective.

> The term "memorizing" is used in the broad sense, based on the Latin root *memor*, meaning "mindful." I use the term "memorize" to mean "to learn by heart," or "to fix in the mind."

As the foreign language is acquired, through very active input, internalization, output, and feedback, fluency develops. As the development level rises, the language learner is able to construct higher level output, which, though entirely composed of the words and phrases acquired through input, differs markedly from that input. Eventually, as the learner becomes fluent in the foreign language, she produces original ideas and astute observations in the second language. Is she simply parroting the input? Is she "regurgitating" what the native language speakers have provided? No—having learned the language, she is able to produce *original* material. As her fluency increases, her level of communicative competence and expressive sophistication rises proportionally.

> Novelist Stephen King explains, "If you want to be a writer, you must do two things above all others: read a lot and write a lot. There's no way around these two things that I'm aware of, no shortcut." King's advice is directly applicable to legal writing as well. Stephen King, *On Writing*, 157.

Basic fluency in a foreign language allows for communication of essential common concepts ("Hello. I am hungry. Where is the market? I need help."). Fluency at a higher level includes the ability to exchange sophisticated thoughts with others and—eventually—the power to persuade others of theoretical positions through rhetoric.

Fluency in the language of the law is achieved precisely the same way—with precisely the same results. Walking into your first class in law school is tantamount to alighting from an airplane in a foreign country, where a foreign language is spoken. The difference is that as you walk through the airport in Mexico City, you notice that just about *everyone* around you is speaking Spanish—immersion is immediate and unavoidable. However, during the first semester of law school, only the professors are speaking the language of the law. But even the professors, since they know they are speaking to an audience of people who do not yet understand the language, speak a gentler version, explaining vocabulary and the logical structure of the language as they lecture. True "immersion" is unavailable during the beginning of your practice.

Therefore, you will have to actively design a method by which you obtain frequent, large, correct, and progressively more sophisticated input, develop a system for internalizing what you take in, and construct strategies to provide adequate output opportunities, complete with feedback. That's what this book is all about—achieving fluency in the language of the law, through active *practice* of law. Development of fluency in the language of the law is essential to attainment of the objectives that most entering law students share:

- A rich, deep foundation for the professional practice of law.
- Grades reflecting the student's personal best effort.
- First-time bar passage.

> As soon as you attain a moderate level of fluency in the language of the law, you will begin to think and write like a lawyer. *Then* you are in a position to get the most out of law school, through continual conversation with your professors and peers about jurisprudential matters of common interest.

Attaining fluency in the language of the law need not take 1000 days—you can expedite the process. You have proven your fundamental aptitude to the satisfaction of your law school—your acceptance into the student body is convincing evidence that a committee of professional educators has assessed your qualifications and determined that you have the ability to learn, write, speak, think, and practice law. The ease of reaching this objective will vary from student to student—just as with foreign language learning, some have an aptitude that facilitates faster learning. The speed with which you accomplish your objective and the degree of competence you achieve depend upon your passion and your persistence.

To achieve fluency in the language of the law, employ the same method outlined above relating to foreign language acquisition: diligently attend to input, internalization, output, and feedback. In law school, you are offered an abundant supply of each—an offering many law students avoid.

Input comes from reading and listening. Your law school opportunities for input include:

- Reading your casebook. Active reading of every sentence within the pages specified in your syllabi—cases, notes, comments, and footnotes—is essential.
- Listening to professors during class. All law professors speak the language of the law. Pay attention to what they say and how they say it. Think of your professors' speech as the model for your own—each class provides a rich opportunity to experience how someone at the highest

levels of fluency employs the language to assist in forming thoughts and to convey both pragmatic and abstract concepts persuasively.

- Reading required, suggested, or available collateral and supportive material. When professors require or suggest that you review books or law review articles other than your casebook, they are providing you with further opportunities to enhance your learning through input. Your library and electronic research sources abound with law review articles offering detailed explanation and analysis of every important aspect of the law. "Hornbooks" constitute another valuable input resource, and are often recommended by professors—your law school library should be well-stocked with hornbooks.

- Reading commercial study aids. All commercial study aids are subject to several caveats: (1) some may contain incorrect law; (2) all cover material beyond what your professor will cover in class; (3) some concentrate heavily on "the law" and little on analysis—students often accept this concentration as a green light to forego development of essential analytical skills—avoid that mistake; (4) some approaches taken by commercial sources conflict with some professors' preferred pedagogic methodology, and may therefore confuse students. Be open to your professors' advice in this regard.

- Listening to students during class. At first, most of your peers will manifest a distinct inability to reason and speak as lawyers do. Mentally engage yourself with every student comment or response and evaluate it (to yourself)—use the successes and mistakes of others to your own learning advantage.

- Listening to recommended audio and videotapes. Your law school bookstore and several commercial bar review courses offer audio and videotapes produced to provide you with explanations of the law and test-taking strategies. These tapes can usually be counted on for their near-perfect use of the language of the law.

> *Hornbooks* are detailed treatises on specific areas of law, written by eminent authorities. The term "hornbook" was used in the fifteenth century, when lessons for children were written on parchment, glued to wooden paddles, and covered with a thin, transparent layer of cow's horn.

> Throughout this book, you will find tips on how to use study aids most effectively. Also, turn to the supplement describing many first-year commercial study aids.

Internalization means fixing the intaken knowledge—facts, data, rules, definitions, theories—within your mind, making it instantly and automatically available. Internalization results from repeated usage of the material, and/or by application of memory techniques.

Output takes place when you speak and write in the language of the law. Your law school opportunities for output include:

- Speaking in class—whether called upon unexpectedly, or in response to your raised hand.
- Discussing law with your fellow students—both informally and quasi-formally during study group sessions.
- Conversing with professors during office visits.
- Writing a course summary (referred to by many students as an "outline").
- Writing a course flow chart.

- Writing responses to practice exams that professors hand out during class.
- Writing responses to practice exams formally archived at your school (usually in the library or on a web site).
- Writing responses to practice exams from other schools.
- Writing responses to bar examination questions.
- Writing responses to short, single-issue, hypothetical questions found in commercial sources.
- Writing responses to questions that fellow students design.
- Writing responses to questions that the school's academic support program offers.
- Completing all writings your professors assign as course requirements (often encountered in Legal Methods or Legal Writing courses).

Feedback consists of evaluative responses to your output. Some feedback is passive and standardized; other feedback is active and personal. The former includes "suggested answers" and "model answers" to which you should compare your work product. Active, personal feedback opportunities include:

- Submitting your practice exam answers to your doctrinal law professors.
- Exchanging practice answers with your colleagues.
- Asking for writing evaluations from second- and third-year students who excelled in the subjects you are taking—either informally or through mentor programs that your school's academic support program offers.
- Seeking writing evaluations from legal writing professors and other professionals affiliated with your school's academic support program.

Does this challenge of achieving fluency in the language of the law seem formidable? It should. You have chosen a profession that demands rigor, determination, and focused attention. In Part Two, you will discover how to begin *working* like a lawyer to prepare you to *think* and *write* like a lawyer. Begin the practice now.

---

[1] Laurie A. Morin. *Reflections on Teaching Law As Right Livelihood: Cultivating Ethics, Professionalism, and Commitment to Public Service from the Inside Out*, 35 Tulsa L. J. 227, 237 (2000).

[2] See *Juggling It All: Exploring Lawyers' Work, Home, and Family Demands and Coping Strategies—Report of Stage One Findings* 5 (Sept. 2002) Law School Admission Council Research Report RR-00-02, Jean Wallace, Department of Sociology, The University of Calgary.

[3] Yon Maley, *The Language of the Law, in Language and the Law* 11 (John Gibbons ed., Longman Group UK Limited 1994).

[4] Anthony G. Amsterdam & Jerome Bruner, *Minding the Law* 34 (Harvard University Press, 2000).

[5] Ruta K. Stropus, *Mend It, Bend It, and Extend It: The Fate of Traditional Law School Methodology in the 21st Century*, 27 Loy. U. Chi. L. J. 449, 471 (1996).

---

6 An example is this statement by the Maryland Bar Examiners: "Bar Admission Rule 7(b) sets out the purpose of the Bar Examination and states in pertinent part: '...the examination shall be designed to test the examinee's knowledge of legal principles in the subjects on which examined and the examinee's ability to recognize, analyze, and intelligibly discuss legal problems and to apply that knowledge in reasoning their solution. The examination will not be designed primarily to test information, memory, or experience.'" *Available at* http://www.courts.state.md.us/ble/examgrading.html (last visited July 2003).

PART TWO

COMPONENTS OF ASSESSMENT-TARGETED STUDY

Lawyers Segment Their Work

Trials are presented in discrete segments: plaintiff's opening statement, defendant's opening statement, plaintiff's case (presentation of evidence), defendant's case, plaintiff's rebuttal, plaintiff's closing argument, defendant's closing argument, plaintiff's rebuttal. Opinion letters are written in several stages: client interview, legal research, initial drafting, further research, redrafting, revising, editing, and proofreading.

> Opinion letters are written by lawyers for clients, to express and explain an educated legal opinion as to the application of a law to a client's situation.

Scrutiny of each step of these processes would reveal another layer of subparts. The defendant's case presented during trial, for example, may include oral testimony by five lay witnesses and one expert witness, cross-examination of a witness previously called to the stand by plaintiff (an "adverse witness"), presentation of an excerpt from a videotaped deposition, introduction into evidence of a replica, and introduction into evidence of a variety of documents.

Lawyers isolate the components of their targeted outcome, and engage in detailed, exhaustive preparation *of each component* to ensure that the product (whether a trial, a will, a tax return, a legislative bill or an appellate brief) represents a totality of their best work. The litigator, for example, will engage in comprehensive and painstaking pre-trial preparation of her cross-examination of an adverse witness. That preparation will likely include:

> A deposition is an out-of-court "discovery" proceeding involving testimony by witnesses responding to questions asked by trial lawyers. The testimony is transcribed by a court reporter or stenographer, and may be used at trial, or in other proceedings.

- Reading, summarizing, indexing, highlighting, excerpting, and studying—even to the point of memorizing portions of—the witness's deposition transcript.
- Pouring over all documents that may have a bearing on the witness's testimony to find topical areas that may be helpful during the cross-examination.
- Discussing with her client (or other friendly witnesses) the highlights of the expected direct testimony, seeking information about how to counter the testimony through cross-examination.
- Brainstorming, often with other lawyers in the firm, to figure out the weaknesses in the witness's anticipated direct testimony and how to make the most of them during cross-examination.
- Investigating the possibility of eliciting information that may impeach (discredit) the witness's credibility.
- Anticipating, through simulation, how the course of the testimony may proceed, including objections by opposing counsel.
- Preparing arguments to overcome any anticipated objections.

To *fractionate* is to divide into discrete parts.

Salient, derived from the Latin word for "jump," is a word law students encounter frequently. It means "prominent," or "of notable significance." Salient facts in a narrative, for example, are those that (metaphorically) "jump out" at the reader.

A *subpoena* is a court order requiring a person to appear and testify. The word derives from two Latin words for "under penalty." Many subpoenas include the words, "Under penalty [of contempt], you are commanded to appear...."

The most effective attorneys focus on their objectives, *fractionate* them, and then intensely prepare to prevail as to each component. Salient features of lawyerly preparation of work product include:

The preparation follows a thoughtful, well-designed plan. Lawyers are experts at planning. The complexity, intensity, and urgency of each enterprise, as well as the gravity of the subject matter and significance of the consequences of the lawyer's work, demand consummate attention to design strategy.

The plan is chronologically and temporally practical. Most steps have prerequisites—a deposition can't be scrutinized until the transcript arrives, the deposition precedes the transcript, the subpoena to appear at the deposition precedes the deposition, the decision as to whom to summon to a deposition precedes the issuance of the subpoena. Every element of the plan must be ordered in a chronologically sensible pattern. Further, the plan must be constructed with due regard for intermediate and ultimate time limits (for example, a fixed trial date).

The design is all-inclusive. The judicious attorney leaves nothing to chance.

Every step of the strategy is focused on the elemental objective. Once the ultimate objective has been separated into its component aspects, each preparatory act should be precisely aimed at the targeted element.

The program is continually scrutinized and adapted. Things change. Prudent lawyers expect to revise their plan of action because of unforeseeable events—therefore, they exercise the executive management skill of regular review and modification. A call from a client, a witness's failure of recollection, a new ruling by the Supreme Court, a settlement offer, a death, passage of a bill through Congress—innumerable *external* developments or forces will necessitate adaptation. Likewise, *internal* occurrences and catastrophes—unanticipated explosion of work in the office, termination of a paralegal, computer glitch—can (and always *do*) intervene and provide ample reason for review and modification of the plan.

Successful Law Students Segment Their Work

Law students who realize that the practice of law begins upon matriculation employ the executive-level managerial characteristics of attorneys by segmenting their work. The most effective law students focus on their objectives, fractionate them, and then intensely prepare to prevail as to each component.

Your first-semester objectives should be consistent with your longer-range goals, and therefore include:

- Developing a comprehensive understanding of each field of law you are studying (usually including Torts, Contracts, Property and Civil Procedure).
- Achieving fluency in the language of each distinct field of law you are studying, as well as attaining a wide-ranging facility in the general language of the law.
- Developing and mastering the skills of lawyering.
- Earning grades as high as your capability allows.

If your objectives approximate these, you will do superbly on law school examinations when you achieve your objectives—because not only will you have achieved the very goals your professors have in mind for you but you will be able to demonstrate your accomplishment on final examinations. As Professor Philip Kissam, from the University of Kansas School of Law explains, when professors read and grade law school examination answers to essay questions, they are assessing students' understanding of the subject matter, "inferential abilities, analytical abilities, and judgment concerning particular legal problems." They look for "sound ... interpretation of events and authorities; demonstration of practical reason, judgment and innovation in developing and reconciling competing arguments or making decisions; and the employment of rhetoric in forming well-constructed and persuasive arguments."[7]

Therefore, if you target personal-best performance on examinations as your goal and if you prepare for those examinations in a lawyerly manner, you will be heading directly toward accomplishing the particular objectives set forth above. Segmenting your work, to provide consistent practice of each element mentioned by Professor Kissam in each subject area, will lead directly to your ultimate objectives.

The Law CATS

The Components of Assessment Targeted Study (CATS) are these:

- Reading and briefing every case.
- Actively attending every class and taking notes.
- Transforming class notes.
- Preparing course summaries.
- Developing flow charts.
- Internalizing.
- Answering practice hypotheticals in writing.

In eduspeak (the language of teachers) tests and examinations are "assessment tools."

Each of the seven Law CATS is an activity mirroring activities practicing lawyers perform each day across the country. If you practice each component assiduously each week during law school, you will be practicing law each week. Here is a brief description of each of the Law CATS:

Reading and Briefing

This compound activity occurs prior to class. "Reading" means active reading—close examination of text, comprehension of the literal meaning, discernment of the relevance of the information within the grand scheme of the subject matter, and commitment of the salient portions to short-term memory. "Briefing" means categorizing and summarizing, in writing.

Actively Attending Every Class and Taking Notes

True "attendance" in class—every class—means so much more than simple presence in the classroom. Active engagement is essential. Exam-targeted note taking is an art. She who keeps a discerning eye on the target during each day's class will take notes with purpose—notes that will substantially enhance her ability to demonstrate her legal skills, knowledge, and fluency on the final examination.

Transforming Class Notes

Raw material is unprocessed product, used in a manufacturing process.

Notes taken during class are raw material, like iron ore mined from the ground. Ore mined from class (and included in class notes) is an essential ingredient in the powerful legal analyses students write in final examinations. Just as the iron ore is raw, requiring substantial processing before becoming useful, so also class notes must undergo functional metamorphosis before they are useful in fabricating the ultimate product.

Preparing Course Summaries

A course summary (often referred to an "outline" by law students and professors) is a personal compilation of the essentials of a course—your self-created Ultimate Authority on each subject. The generative process of course summary production, you will quickly learn, is more important than the product produced. That explains why no other student's outline or course summary, or any commercial summary, can possibly take the place of your own.

> Again, adverting to the Latin, *ultimate* is derived from *ultimare*, "to come to an end." The course summary is where the essential info gathering stops.

Developing Flow Charts

Careful extraction of topical words and phrases from your personal course summary will provide you with a hierarchical outline of the course, providing a pre-developed structure for analytical presentation of a cogent legal argument in each thematic category. Construction of flow charts adds dynamism, direction, and schematic arrangement, as well as providing inestimable memory stimulation value—especially for kinesthetic, visual, and tactile learners.

> Kinesthetic learners learn better by writing information, by becoming physically involved in problem resolving. Tactile learners learn better by manipulating information. Visual learners need to "see" the schematic relationships between blocks of information.

Internalizing (Memorizing)

To "memorize" is to "learn by heart," to fix firmly in the mind. Internalization takes place when that which is so learned, so "fixed," merges with what already exists in our minds, adding to the skein of cognitive yarn from which we weave the fabric of our analytical propositions and arguments. The term "memorize" within this context of law study refers to the total process—including both aspects, "fixing" and "merging." The former, without the latter, is useless.

Answering Practice Hypotheticals in Writing

Nearly every law school examination includes hypothetical fact situations, ending with a directive enjoining the students to identify and deal with the legal issues that the narrative suggests. Practice at this particular exercise, usually the sole determiner of your grade, is essential. The Royal Shakespeare Company practices; the New York Yankees practice; Venus Williams practices; Tara Lipinski practices. What they all practice most is the very activity they intend to be judged on. For you, that event is answering hypotheticals in writing—your final examination.

> *Hypothetical* derives from the Greek word *hupotithenai*, "to suppose." When professors deliver "hypotheticals" orally, in class, they often start with the word "Suppose ...," followed by a made-up series of facts. The word "suppose" is omitted from the facts presented on final exams—nevertheless, the format remains the same. Thus, the use of the term "hypothetical" to designate the narratives constituting the basis of most first-year law exams (and bar examinations).

Segmenting Your Work to Include All the CATS Weekly—Planning

Segmenting your work simply amounts to making sure that each study week includes each of the CATS for each of your subjects. In other words, for Torts, you should plan to spend several hours each week "studying," but that "study" should be divided into class attendance and six other discrete activities—the rest of the CATS. The key word here is "plan"—because of the volume of work, the variety of subject matter, and the anxieties inherent in this foray into an alien culture. Covering all the bases without significant forethought is, at best, rather difficult. Efficient planning is best accomplished proactively, methodically and quantitatively, and it is goal-specific.

Proactive planning is anticipatory. Proactive planning assumes a wary attitude of active cognizance of the problems inherent in studying law, coupled with the information and drive necessary to thwart their interference with attainment of your goal.

Methodical planning is systematic. The method you apply to planning your Torts study strategy—with slight adjustments—will work equally well for Civil Procedure.

Quantitative planning is based on measurement—in this case, the measurement of available time, overlaid on a measurement of material to be covered.

Goal-specific planning is targeted. Ideal goal-specific planning assures that each component of the plan directly assists in attainment of the goal, as an essential element of the ultimate work product or as a positive catalyst to its production.

> A *catalyst* is a substance that causes a change in the rate of a chemical reaction—catalysts are used in many industrial applications. They work by changing a reaction's activation energy. Substances that *increase* the reaction rate are called *positive catalysts*. Learning catalysts increase your rate of progressing toward your ultimate objectives.

> An *equestrian* is a person exceptionally skilled in riding, caring for, and understanding horses.

How Planning and Practice Work Together

Suppose you signed up for a class entitled "Thinking Like an Equestrian," that you have no horseback experience whatsoever and are actually afraid of horses. The course includes lectures and required readings on related topics: horse health, horse training, the history of horses, riding techniques, and horse psychology. The syllabus explains that the course objectives, including total understanding of everything about horses, will be assessed by a single performance exam—at the end of the semester, you must select a horse from several in the corral, mount the horse bareback, and ride 25 miles through forests, hills, and streams, completing the ride in three hours.

Which method of preparation for the ultimate course assessment do you suppose would net you the highest grade?

Method One—The passive method. If you were to employ the passive method for this course, you would read each of the required books, highlight many significant paragraphs, attend all of the lectures, take notes, rewrite your notes, discuss horses for long hours with your study group, talk about how you would resolve horse performance problems, watch someone ride a horse, and fret. For this three-credit course, you may spend as much as 12 hours each week studying (in addition to class time) because you find it very difficult to understand the subject matter.

Method Two—The active method. Employing this method, you would read each of the assigned books, attend every lecture, take notes, extract essential information from your notes, and ride horses. For example, the first week, you would approach a horse and talk to it daily; the second week, while talking to the horse, you would also groom it; the third week, you would add mounting the horse and riding very slowly in an enclosed area; the fourth week, you would ride a little faster; by week seven, you would be riding several hours in a corral, ready to venture out into the forest trails. Each week, you will have selected a different horse, so you will become familiar with a variety of temperaments and gaits. All the reading and listening you will be doing (in class and in the library) will make much more sense to you as your riding proficiency progresses. By week ten, you should be ready for your first very long trail ride. You will have fallen from horses several times by the twelfth week, but by then you will have realized that if you hop right back on the animal and proceed with aplomb, you will reach your objective quite handily. During the week before the final assessment (the performance test) you may ride a horse 25 or 30 miles every other day. On "exam day," you will be filled with well-deserved self-confidence, and you will be ready to ride.

The first method (passive) focuses on this: reading, discussing, and attempting to comprehend a complex subject matter completely out of context, while avoiding the difficult task of learning how to *use* the information.

The second method focuses on this: a deep, rich, comprehensive understanding of horses and horsemanship and the development of equestrian skills at a high level, both of which will be assessed by a practical performance test under strict time constraints.

The analogy is only clear when you understand this: law professors expect their students to attain a deep, rich, comprehensive understanding of the law and to develop the analytical, problem-resolving skills of a lawyer, at a high level, to be assessed by a practical performance test under strict time constraints.

To *excel* in resolving sticky legal problems in writing, under time pressure, a student must *practice* resolving sticky legal problems in writing, under time pressure—the more the better.

Will you be "ready to ride?"

Component 1
Read and Brief Every Case

Practicing Lawyers Read and Brief

Despite the fact that Susan Mahaffey, the most recent lawyer to join the staff at Manzano, Kingsley & Apple, had arisen at 5:30 a.m., already run her daily three miles, and driven through busy morning traffic to reach the firm before 8:00, she still looked forward to that first cup of coffee to kick her into full throttle. As she poured the dark, aromatic, freshly ground beans into the brown paper filter, she was startled by the strength of Jillian Manzano's business-like, "Good morning."

"Thanks for making the coffee, Sue. The phone was ringing when I arrived an hour ago, and I've been on that same call ever since. Remember I told you about the accountant who said he was going to refer that building contractor to the firm? Well, it was the contractor on the phone. It sounds as though we may need to get to court right away and ask for an injunction." As usual, Jillian talked quickly. She expected whoever was listening to fill in the blanks between her thoughts—it was as though she assumed that her audience was as familiar with the subject as she.

Jillian continued to speak, as the water dribbled through the filter, producing a thick substance resembling coffee more in fragrance than viscosity. Susan had once again ground the beans too fine and not added enough water. She admitted often that she had no future as a chef.

"He acquainted me with his situation. I jotted it all down on this legal pad." With that, the taller woman handed the yellow tablet to Susan. "See if you can figure out what the applicable law is—I'm not sure if state or federal law applies here—and let me know what to tell the client when he swings by the office after lunch."

Susan knew precisely what Jillian Manzano expected—a memo—a three or four-page explanation setting forth the precise statutes and cases that would determine how the client's problems would be resolved. Jillian knew she could count on Susan to discern which components of the convoluted story scribbled on the legal pad were the most pertinent and to explain why and how those facts interwove with the law. She knew Susan would provide her with a well-reasoned and correct explanation of how the law would affect the client's circumstances.

As she approached the firm's library, Susan thought of the many cases she had briefed throughout law school. She smiled as she realized that this morning, she was doing precisely what she had practiced for years in school—legal research, case briefing, and legal writing. For each case she mentioned in her memo, she would provide Jillian with the case citation, touch on the case history, detail the salient facts, and explain how the court reasoned to its conclusion, its ultimate decision, its "holding." Each holding would provide a precedent Susan would rely on in structuring her analysis of the new client's position.

During her second semester at school, Susan recalled, many of her friends had chided her for continuing to brief every case in her casebooks. "Haven't you caught on yet," they'd explain, "all you need to do is 'book brief,' Sue. Just highlight the issue in one color, and the holding in another; put a few notes in the margin, and you're done! You spend too much time writing out briefs. Take the shortcut."

Her fellow students were right about one thing—briefing was time-consuming work. But as the months went by, she developed a facility for extracting the essential elements from the long court opinions, and the chore of briefing became systematic. In a weird sense, she mused, it had almost become fun. She knew this morning that without all that practice at distilling the essential ingredients from appellate opinions, practice at separating the wheat from the chaff, practice at digesting lengthy legal arguments, she would not be able to write the brief Jillian Manzano expected to see on her desk in four hours.

Stretching to reach a volume of the Supreme Court Reporter on the top shelf, Susan turned to acknowledge the entrance of Mike Kingsley, another of the firm's senior partners.

"Nice coffee, Susan—thanks! Who taught you to make it so strong? I haven't had a cup like this since the last time I was in Paris. Why don't you show the others how you do it?"

> A *loophole* is an inadvertent omission or ambiguity in the language of a document or statute that provides a means of avoiding compliance.

Lawyers read interminably, deeply, thoroughly, thoughtfully, slowly, seriously, attentively, observantly, precisely, meticulously, painstakingly. Folklore has it that they read to find "loopholes." Actually, they read to find similarities, differences, distinctions, and categorizations; they read to understand complex and often subtle analytical arguments; in short, they read to comprehend and internalize the material.

Start Practicing Now: Read and Brief Every Case

The reading that you will be doing in law school is nearly identical to the reading you will be doing as a lawyer. The better you become at it during your three years of practice during law school, the better you will be at it when you begin the professional practice.

Reading legal material almost never allows for "skimming" or quick reading … rather, it requires an intensive, often physically exhausting search for answers to questions. The questions are usually those raised *before* the actual reading begins. When a civil rights lawyer reads a Supreme Court opinion to determine whether it can be distinguished from the case she's currently working on, she reads it in detail. When a tax lawyer reads a convoluted series of sections of the Internal Revenue Code, she can't afford to breeze through the statutes, getting the "gist" of them. Both lawyers have been hired by their clients because of their capabilities to read and comprehend dense legal material.

When you read for your class preparation, practice development of the same professional capability—become an expert at comprehending all the meaning packed into the complicated and intricately constructed legal texts you will be faced with for the duration of your career.

If your objective is to achieve fluency in the language of the law, recognize that reading is the main source of language input—the more you read, the more input you will be receiving. The more *active* your reading is, the more *active* (and thus, effective) your cognitive language-learning apparatus will be functioning.

But law students often complain that they have too much reading to do—they believe they *need* to "skim" or "book brief" or not brief cases at all, due to lack of time. The reason they harbor this delusion is simple: they believe they are still in "school"—they have not yet begun to practice law. If you take the time to learn the mechanics of reading and briefing cases, you will quickly develop a heightened efficiency. The second-semester student who complains of not having enough time to read her Civil Procedure assignment entirely, or to brief all her Criminal Law cases, or to comprehend the complexities presented in her Constitutional Law text is most likely the same student who did not struggle through the first few weeks, slowly learning the most effective methods for in-depth reading and comprehension of this complex material. For some students the skill develops more easily than for others—for all students it is essential if they are to achieve their parallel and complementary goals of obtaining grades reflective of their "personal best" and preparing most effectively for the professional practice of law.

And lawyers brief. When they write a respondent's appellate brief, a memorandum of points and authorities in support of a demurrer, or a letter to a client clarifying why her adoption papers must remain confidential, lawyers explain and support their positions by summarizing written opinions rendered by appellate courts in cases which dealt with issues similar to those about which they are writing. These summaries bear remarkable resemblance to the "briefs" law students produce daily as part of their class preparation.

Throughout law school, you will be required to produce written material to be scrutinized by professors (appellate arguments, research papers, examination answers), but the fundamental writing activity produces a product no one but you will ever see. That activity is briefing. Despite the fact that you are the exclusive audience for this writing, it is nevertheless the most important foundational writing you will do in law school. Strong brief-writing skills develop into strong exam-writing skills, and generate the strong writing skills excellent lawyers manifest. As Professor James Moliterno and Frederic Lederer, of The College of William and Mary School of Law, point out:

> *The relationship between the writing you will do in law school writing or skill courses and the writing you will do as a lawyer is clear: they produce the same kinds of documents. What may be less clear, but equally important, is the relationship between the law school exams, outlines, and casebriefs you will write and the writing you will do in practice. The exams, outlines, and casebriefs are not only important vehicles for learning the law, they are also opportunities to practice the process of legal analysis that will find its way into all of your writing as a lawyer.*[8]

Remember, lawyers with experience are reading and writing in a language in which they enjoy fluency. As one just beginning on the career path, you are working *toward* that fluency. Before your reading and briefing capabilities are sharpened by practice, you can expect to experience difficulty comprehending and digesting the dense material you encounter in your casebooks. You need to approach it systematically.

The primary material law students (and most lawyers) read consists of "cases." Before you read a case or brief a case, you need to know what a "case" is and what a law student's "briefing" of that case is all about. Here's an explanation of both.

About "Cases"

The "briefs" lawyers file in appellate courts are not the same as "briefs" law students prepare for class. Law student "briefs" each summarize only one court opinion. "Briefs" filed in courts are detailed arguments supporting legal positions.

Usually, a lawsuit begins in the *trial court*, where it is resolved by the trial judge (sometimes with the assistance of a jury). If one of the parties to the litigation believes the trial judge erred in that phase, the party may *appeal* to a "higher" court, a *court of appeal*.

The *court of appeal* reviews written arguments submitted by the *appellant* or *petitioner* (the appealing party) and the *appellee* or *respondent* (the responding party). Along with the written arguments (these are referred to as *briefs*), the *justices* (appellate court terminology for "judges") may review transcripts of testimony and documents introduced as evidence during the trial. The attorneys for the litigants often accept invitations to appear before the appellate court to state their positions orally (at *hearings*) and to respond to questions from the justices. However, no *trial* takes place during this appellate phase—no witnesses are called and no jury is present.

The appellate court's focus is always on how the *law* should be applied to the facts of the particular case. Sometimes, appellate courts need to interpret vague statutes or earlier muddled expressions of law; other times, although the law may be clear, the facts of the case may allow for the application of one of several conflicting legal principles. From time to time, appellate courts seize the opportunity of deciding a particular case as an opportunity to change the law or the way the law is applied.

> The reviewing court evaluates the trial judge's handling of a range of legal issues, like admissibility of evidence or rulings on motions made by the lawyer who lost at trial.

One of the justices expresses the court's ruling in a written *opinion*. An appellate opinion usually sets forth:

- The pertinent facts of the case.
- A statement of the *issues* (the legal points the litigants are disputing).
- The applicable laws (often referred to as the *rules*).
- The court's *rationale* (the reasoning which supports the court's decision).
- The *holding* (the statement of the court's decision in the case, in terms of the legal claim and the important facts).
- The procedural result (for example, whether the case will be *remanded* —sent back—to the trial court for another trial).

This written "opinion" of the court of appeal is a "case." In law school, most of your reading will be from casebooks—heavily edited and annotated collections of these "cases."

Nuts and Bolts: Briefing Cases

When you *brief a case* in law school, you are summarizing the facts, rule, rationale, holding, and result of an appellate opinion. Law students brief cases for a variety of reasons. Professor Paul Bateman, from Southwestern University School of Law, explains why briefing is important:

> *To participate fully in [the classroom] experience, the tool you need is a thoughtful brief to navigate through the day's discussion. Furthermore, since comfort level in class is essential to your socialization to the study of law, a good set of case briefs for each class becomes an essential component for providing that comfort level. Moreover, your comfort level can be raised further once your briefs allow you to overcome one of the major*

causes of law student stress—lack of concrete feedback. A case brief provides a self-assessment tool that can help you monitor class discussion, and so provide you with feedback about your understanding of the legal concept being discussed.[9]

Professors call on students during class and expect them to be able to discuss the particulars of the assigned cases in detail. Briefing helps students comprehend the opinions, and the written brief provides a handy (and welcome) set of notes to refresh student recollection during class. (That is what Professor Bateman is addressing when he refers to the "comfort level.")

Preparing briefs is more than preparing for individual classes—more than abating anxiety. Keep in mind that your first day in class is your first formal day of preparation for the practice of law. "The process [of case briefing]," one law student resource points out, "is one that is basic to lawyers' work."[10] Litigators, tax attorneys, legislators, corporate counsel, legal scholars—most lawyers must be adept at closely reading court opinions, analyzing and summarizing them, and applying them.

What is included in a *case brief*? Since the only "audience" for a student's brief is the author of that brief, each student's brief will (and should) differ; and each student may produce different style briefs for different classes. Some instructors may expect students to delve deeply into the facts of each case, while others may be more concerned with the relationships among several cases in the field. Your civil procedure professor, for example, will be *very* concerned about the *procedural history* of the case (how and why it wound up in the appellate process), and may require considerable attention to details involving the *residence* of the parties to the lawsuit, the *amount in controversy*, and other particulars. Your Torts professor, however, may be much more interested in the social consequences of a particular line of legal reasoning. Generally, a law student's brief should generally include these items:

> The citation also includes the series, volume number, and page where lawyers can find the case in the "court reports," the bound volumes of court opinions that you will find in the law library. Adding citations to your briefs is not essential for class preparation but *is* for research projects.

- *Citation.* A case's "citation" includes the names of the parties, the court deciding the case, and the year of the decision. It is helpful to include the page on which the case appears in the textbook as well.
- *Parties.* Each brief should include the names and circumstances of each party to the underlying lawsuit. Who sued whom? Who won at trial? Which party is the *appellant*? What are the relative positions or relationships between the parties? Is one party the landowner and the other the tenant? Did the *plaintiff* (the person or entity who sued the defendant in the trial court) employ the *defendant*? Is one party a *minor*?
- *Relief sought and disposition.* When the case was filed in the trial court, the plaintiff was asking the court for a particular *award*, *order*, or *judgment* of some kind. What was it? How did the trial court dispose of

the case? Who won or lost what? What is the *appellant* asking the appellate court to do? If this case has been appealed more than once, what happened last time?

- *Legal theories*. When the parties appeared in the trial court, the plaintiff asserted certain facts and asked the court to apply particular laws, to reach a favorable result. The defendant proffered a defense—either a different version of the facts or a different legal theory. In your brief, you need to summarize their positions. The party who lost at trial usually claims—in her appeal—that the trial court erroneously interpreted or applied the law. In your brief, you should describe this position and the legal contention of the appellee (the party resisting the appeal—that is, the party who won at trial) as well.

- *Signigicant facts*. Not all the facts adduced during a trial are of legal significance on appeal. The significant facts are those that are necessary to explain the relationship of the parties, particularly with respect to their legal positions on appeal. Would changing or eliminating a fact change the result of the case? If so, the fact is significant. These legally significant facts are also referred to by some courts, professors and authors as *key* facts, *operative* facts, *material* facts, and *salient* facts. As set forth in your brief, the facts should seldom be longer than several short phrases or sentences.

- *Issue*. The issue is the question of law (including the key facts) to be answered by the appellate court. Often, several issues are presented to the court—however, the cases in most of your casebooks have been heavily edited so that issues extraneous to the particular topic being studied are deleted from the version you read. If several issues are included, does resolution of one issue depend on how another is resolved first? If so, the first issue to be resolved is referred to as a *threshold* issue. Because the court's expression of an issue may not be the best expression for law student purposes, in your brief you should try to rewrite each issue in the form of a question that can be answered "yes" or "no." A good statement of the issue will explain the legal question in one sentence, understandable to someone who has not read the case. This concise issue statement is important because law professors often ask students to "identify the issue" in a case, orally, during class. They expect students to refer to their briefs, either to read directly from them or to use them as guides for recitation of the issue. Usually, that issue is the focal point of the day's class—so framing the issue carefully is a matter of great importance.

- *Holding*. When the court reaches a conclusion, it is usually presented as an answer to the question raised by the *issue*. That answer is the court's holding. One way to state the holding of a case is to turn around the question that is the *issue* and make it a declarative sentence—thus answering the question in terms of the facts of the case that raised the issue.

> "Law school shorthand" is a term many law students use to describe a host of abbreviations law students often use in briefing and note-taking: P for Plaintiff, J for Judgment, and K for Contract are a few. Type "law school shorthand" into an Internet search engine to find more information.

- *Rule.* The court reaches its holding by applying a legal principle to the facts. That legal principle is the *rule*. Consider whether the case you are reading tends to broaden or limit the rule (by, for example, limiting the application of the rule to certain circumstances), or represents an exception to a general rule.
- *Rationale.* The part of the court opinion that lays out the reasoning of the court is the *rationale*—a tightly woven explanation of how the court reached its conclusion, the rationale provides a model for students to emulate in their legal reasoning.
- *Dictum.* Often used in its plural form (*dicta*), this Latin word is short for *obiter dictum*, literally meaning "something said in passing." *Dictum* is an observation of a judge that has only incidental bearing on the case in question and is not essential to the determination of the case. Although *dictum* is not legally binding for future cases, it may be instructive or persuasive when other courts consider the same issue in later years, and it may foreshadow trends or tendencies of the court. Be prepared to separate *dictum* from the *holding* of the case.
- *Separate opinions.* Many appellate court opinions are followed by *dissenting* or *concurring* opinions. These opinions are written by justices who disagree with the majority of the court or who agree but wish to express a different rationale for their decision or otherwise comment on the main text of the court's opinion. Many professors expect students to familiarize themselves with these separate opinions—often they provide the catalyst for discussion.
- *Appellate Disposition.* The "disposition" mentioned above relates to how the case was determined in the trial court. Likewise, the appellate court will make a ruling (for example, affirming or reversing the trial court). Your professor will expect you to be aware of this disposition. Note it in your brief.

Policies are underlying social or public standards and goals. Some examples of policies courts may consider include efficient administration of justice, economic considerations, ethical issues, freedom of the press, equal protection under the law, or national security questions. Behind every set of laws, and behind every judicial decision, a policy lurks.

These standard elements of student briefs are detailed and explained at The University of Dayton School of Law Professor Vernellia Randall's website (http://academic.udayton.edu.legaled/online/). Professor Randall's pages also include superb advice on a comprehensive panoply of study-skill topics. Spend some time browsing and learning.

Despite the inclusion of all that material in a brief, the product itself should not be long. After all, it is a "brief." How long is a brief? A single-spaced, two-page, 10-point font, typed brief is not brief. The format you adopt should promote concision. You should learn to read a case with an "eye" trained to recognize into which "section" of your brief a particular passage or line fits. Systematically, quickly and precisely mark each case *as you read it* so that the passages relating to each section of your brief are easily identified and brought together in a concise and accurate manner when you actually write the brief. How? Employ the variant of the SQ3R method recommended below.

Simply repeating everything in the court's opinion is unproductive and of no value; only record enough information to trigger your recollection of what the court said. Write the brief in such a way that you will be able to read and comprehend it long after you have put the book away—you will be returning to many of these briefs for later study sessions when you begin writing your course summary.

Reading and Briefing Every Case Effectively and Efficiently

Law students who are practicing law read and brief cases with acute perception, discernment, and understanding. The SQ3R method,[11] adapted to law study—to incorporate briefing—is a perfect method for this type of reading. The acronym SQ3R results from the first letters of these active verbs: Survey, Question, Read, Recite, Review. Here is how to use the SQ3R method to read and brief court opinions in your casebook.

Survey—the pre-reading activity

You need to have some idea where the material you are about to read "fits" in the greater scheme of the subject matter. "Surveying" the text provides context. Before you delve into the heavy verbiage of a court's opinion:

- Quickly (five to ten minutes for a typical one-class assignment) survey the entire reading assignment, in order to prepare for what is coming. Look up the main topic in the Table of Contents. See what surrounds it—figure out the lay of the land.
- Review the casebook headings, topics, and subtopics within the pages you are about to read. Look only at whatever is bold-faced, italicized, numbered or underlined.
- Quickly read a brief summary of the topic in a commercial outline or hornbook, if available. Familiarize yourself (don't memorize) with the basic rules and definitions you find.

Many legal educators suggest this third step be avoided—because the *learning* comes from the *struggling* involved in figuring out what the case stands for without any assistance. Consider skipping this step unless you find it is essential.

Question—the initial reading activity

Questioning helps you to read efficiently and effectively. Before you begin reading any difficult material in depth, you should formulate questions about the reading. When you are reading court opinions, those questions are pre-determined by your briefing format (see above). Your questions will be: What are the salient facts; what issue is the court grappling with; what rule of law does the court apply; what are the reasons the court uses to justify its conclusion; how was the case resolved? You will undoubtedly include other questions, depending on the depth of preparation required by each course.

Read—the fundamental reading activity

Active reading helps you comprehend the material and prepare to write your brief. Before you begin to read, put away those highlighters (these highlighting markers lull most students into a false sense of "having been there"—their tracks are misinterpreted by most readers' brains as evidence of active reading; in fact, reading while highlighting is truly passive reading). With pencil in hand, read the case slowly, once, to answer your questions.

- Read actively: visualize the parties to the lawsuit—bring their dispute to life in your mind.
- As you read, jot simple marginal indicators (for example, an "I" for the issue, an "ROL" for the rule of law) in your casebook.
- Re-read only the portions of material you have marked. Then, read a bit more, if necessary, so that you are convinced you have understood the case as a whole and that you understand how the parts interrelate. Until you become fluent in the language of the law, the reading process will seem slow to you; you may need to read paragraphs several times to fully understand them. Don't worry. As you gain fluency you will also become more efficient.

Recite—the post-reading activity

Reciting aloud, while writing your brief, helps you comprehend and analyze the material, prepare your brief, and begin the transfer of ideas from short-term to long-term memory.

Even if you are not alone, actually vocalize the words—silently. This taps into a different area of your brain, helping "fix" the material more permanently. Practice answering questions you anticipate your professor may ask about the case.

- Recite the elements that should appear in your brief, as answers to the questions you formulated—go ahead and look at the text of the court opinion as necessary. Don't simply read the text of the opinion aloud—rather, recite only the few essential words or phrases that will appear in your brief, and rework them as necessary, so that you are not copying the verbiage of the court.
- Write the brief as you recite, by answering the predetermined questions mentioned under "Question" (above).

Review—the post-reading, post-briefing activity

Reviewing the material you have just actively read helps you remember the material longer, rethink the possible answers to your initial questions, and decide what adjustments need to be made to your brief.

As you end a reading session, revisit the table of contents to be certain how the material "fits in."

- Quickly reread the areas of the opinion that you initially flagged with pencil notations.

- Review your brief, to assure yourself you have adequately reflected the essentials of the material you read.
- Adjust your brief as necessary.

As modified for legal reading, the SQ3R method avoids all three of the most prevalent first-year pitfalls—skimming, passive reading, and over-reading (reading all or portions of cases over and over, wasting precious time). After you have read and briefed your assignment, you are ready for the second component: attending class actively and taking notes.

Component 2
Actively Attend Every Class and Take Notes

Practicing Lawyers Never Miss Court

"Richard," the voice on the other end of the phone line began, "I'm calling to find out what happened at the hearing on our client's summary judgment motion this morning in Department Six." Richard, a first-year associate with the small personal injury litigation firm of Bennet and Gonzales, recognized the voice on the cell phone and cringed a bit, thinking of just how to respond.

"Well, Mr. Bennet, I'm not really sure."

"Oh," the partner replied, "I suppose Judge Doldrin took it under submission; is that it?" Bennet and his associate were well aware that Judge Doldrin often declined to rule on motions as important as this one while everyone was still in court, preferring instead to give the matter more thought after the oral arguments of counsel, then sending out a written memorandum of his decision several days after the hearing.

"Well," Richard hesitated, cleared his throat, and stumbled through the next sentence, "You see, Mr. Bennet, I didn't actually go to the hearing. I slept in this morning."

(The story ends here, because the dénouement is not worth writing— it's too easy to figure out. Get the picture?)

It's probably a mistake to suggest that no practicing lawyer ever misses a court appearance. Search your state's case digests under the heading "malpractice" and you will probably find a few examples of this behavior. But believe this: unexcused failure to appear for a hearing, a trial, or even an appointment falls below the minimum standard of acceptable professional law practice.

Just as importantly, lawyers don't simply show up—they show up prepared and alert, and remain engaged throughout the proceeding. Members of the bar cannot afford to be daydreaming when opposing counsel asks an objectionable question during a hearing or scores a rhetorical point with a jury. Lawyers who win cases cannot afford to let their minds wander when witnesses are relating the details of the conversations they overheard or describing their state of mind at the time of the crime, the tort, the contract, the stock solicitation, or the board meeting. Practicing law professionally means active involvement in all phases of every element of the practice.

Start Practicing Law Now: Actively Attend
Every Class and Take Notes

First, the *every* part. Never miss class. As you read through this book, you should come to understand why borrowing your roommate's notes won't suffice, how listening to a tape recording of the class does not even approach live attendance and engagement, and why a near flawless attendance record is essential.

Here's why.

Actively attending every class leads to actively learning the law. "Learn" is an *active* verb. You can't learn at the level you need in law school without activity. In law school, that activity is *dialectic*.

The teaching methods used in most first year law school classes are based upon what law professors refer to as the "Socratic method." Perhaps you read some *Socratic dialogues* when you studied philosophy in college. In these Socratic dialogues, Plato, himself a great teacher, wrote instructive texts about philosophical concepts by presenting a series of conversations in which his teacher, Socrates, engaged the minds of some of the other citizens of Athens in pursuit of general philosophical fundamental truths. Socrates used a cross-examination process, in which he would pose a series of questions to his conversation partners; the inquiries resulted in a chain of questions and answers that usually led the other person to a contradiction of his original idea. As frustrating as this was to Socrates' friends, it seemed to be an extraordinarily effective tool for the great philosopher to lead his associates to higher levels of understanding. His objective was not confusion. His objective was to engage these conversants in *active learning* sessions—and thereby to actually teach them without writing the answers on the blackboard (or the stone tablet) in front of them.

Likewise, the objectives of law professors who employ this vexing but fruitful method of engagement are not frustration and confusion, although those are often the intellectual plateaus which most students (like Socrates' interlocutors) encounter on the path to comprehension.

Through an active classroom dialectic process, law students are able to form universal definitions and arrive at general principles of law by accepting the lead of experts (law professors) along a path of propositions derived through discussion of individual cases. That path leads the discerning student to generalizations and clarity. That same path leads the passive student to confusion.

Students who are underprepared or who fail to *actively* engage in the dialectic process walk out of class asking, "What was she talking about?" and "Why doesn't she ever answer any of our questions?" "How are we

> *Dialectic* is the practice of pursuing the truth—or arriving at the sensible resolution of difficult logical problems—by the exchange of logical arguments.

supposed to learn anything," they inquire, "if all she does is *ask questions*?" Other students will gather in the common area and complain to each other, "Professor Jurice just doesn't know how to teach. Now, I had a professor at Low Expectation College who knew how to teach—after we read a chapter, she'd come into class and outline the whole chapter on the board, then go over it with us, then ask us, 'Do you have any questions.' We always did, and she'd always answer them. Professor Jurice could take a lesson from *her*."

Plato regarded dialectic as the highest of human arts. So do many first-year law professors. Law professors emulate the Socratic method by breaking down abstract ideas into smaller parts, then delving into each part through a series of confounding questions. In this process, there are not many "wrong" answers, but there are responses or comments that are inapposite—that is, off track, or off the path that the professor would like the students to travel. These, the law professor often dismisses casually or nearly ignores, as her eyes roam around the class for a hand attached to someone who may have an answer (or make a point) that is on the right track—even though it may be contradictory to what the professor herself sees as the ultimately desirable result of the discussion. Professors recognize that contradictions in thought are often essential steps to comprehension.

When Plato wrote the Socratic dialogues, he was careful to include a small number of conversational partners. The admissions officers at law schools answer to different authorities. Therefore, (during your first year) you won't encounter the luxury of a handful of intelligent and informed law students engaging in the dialectic process, but rather, dozens, scores, perhaps more than a hundred. How then, can one fully participate in a pedagogic method designed for under a dozen people, in such an environment?

Treat every question as if it is asked of you

Of course, keep in mind, there are as many variations in the classroom methods of professors as there are professors. Adjust.

Most class sessions include a series of questions. "Ms. Keller, would you please share with us the facts of the *Palsgraf* case?" Most questions will be more esoteric: "What is the court driving at here?" Some will be impossible: "So?" Most of these questions will be asked of others. Treat every question as if it is asked of *you*. Formulate an answer. Then measure your answer against every aspect of the response of the student actually called upon. As you do, you will keep apace of the flow of the dialectic; you will actively engage in the weaving of the fabric of the ultimate argument. You will be ready for the moment when the professor unexpectedly calls upon you, and you will be ready to raise your hand to offer an apropos comment during the class period.

Some answers proffered by other students will baffle you. Do not be intimidated. These responses usually fall into one of these categories: unintelligible, poorly expressed, inapposite, or profound. The trick is figuring out which category the response belongs in. Here's how to handle those answers:

- *The unintelligible response and the poorly expressed response.* If the answer seems garbled, see if you can figure out what the student *meant* to express, and then (silently) express it yourself. You will be developing and exercising mental muscles you will need for decades to come in the professional practice—clients, witnesses (and yes, lawyers and judges) will provide you with never-ending opportunities to sort through questions, comments, and answers which you will need to unravel to comprehend. Start practicing now.

- *The inapposite response.* If the student comment seems irrelevant, illogical, inconsequential, way off the mark, or far-fetched, measure the distance from irrelevance to relevance. How far off the mark is the answer and why? You will be surprised by the number of times a peer will respond to a question with a comment that you believe is truly off-the-wall and downright interplanetary, and your professor will say, "Did everyone hear that? Now we're getting to the meat of this case."

> Do not be too quick to dismiss something as out of bounds. If you are unsure—that is, it *seems* irrelevant, but maybe it isn't—pay attention to the professor's handling of the remark, and you should be able to tell.

- *The profound response.* You are not in this alone, and some of your classmates will have reactions and ideas that plumb deeper depths than you have imagined exist in a given area. Translate this: from time to time you will get out-thunk. Savor the moment. One of the most wonderful aspects of law school is this: it attracts some very bright people who bring to the room substantial cultural and experiential diversity, and therefore, a wide range of comprehension, and expression. These are people you are paying lots of money to learn from. It's not all happening from behind the professor's podium—in a superb classroom, it is happening all around you.

But what if you do not understand the remark? What if the professor makes it clear that the student has hit upon something wonderful and you can't begin to figure out what it is, where it comes from, or why it's wonderful? Write it down. Recreate the comment as well as you can, then put the student's name in the margin of your notes. Most of all, do not let the "profound" responses intimidate you. Face it: some students will have better ideas, faster comprehension or more capability in a particular area than you. Treat it as a fact of life, not a fear factor.

> This is a note you should deal with after class. Including the student's name in your notes will provide an adequate reference point for you later—below, in the sections on note-taking and note transformation, you will find methods for handling the comment after class.

When you leave each class, you should be as mentally invigorated and exhausted as you would be after an hour-long lively, challenging conversation with an expert in your chosen professional field. Not only will you have (mentally) responded to every single question your professor poses, but you also will have benefited from the replies of other members of your class—some on the path, some off; some consistent, some controversial, some contradictory. You will have measured each response against your own, then listened to the evaluations (expressed or implied) by your colleagues and the professor. In short, you will have been mentally *active*. As a result, you should be mentally fatigued.

Every classroom experience is a practice session for the very skills you will need to use to score well on final exams, to pass the bar examination the first time around, and to maintain an exemplary professional practice. Total engagement in each practice session—treating every question as if it were asked of you—will provide you with essential training and practice for all three of these objectives.

Maintain professional protocol

Optimum active engagement in the dialectic process of the practice of law requires a different set of classroom protocols and strategies than students have maintained in their early educative experiences. Classroom etiquette, propriety, protocol, decorum, and strategy—no matter what you call it—amounts to targeted behavioral precepts or norms. If law school is designed for the practice of law, the classroom is the practice courtroom within which the aspirants to the bar exercise and develop their professional skills. The law classroom is the inchoate lawyers' analogue to the athletes' gymnasium, the dancers' studio, the astronauts' simulated cockpit, the actors' rehearsal hall. It is serious business for those who plan to win the trial, score the points, dance the dance, orbit the planet, impress the critics.

Sit in the zone

Each law school, and every class within it, will differ as to seating arrangements; however, most schools allow students to select their own seats. Often, those seats become the students' seats for the semester because the professor will maintain a seating chart for purposes of keeping track of attendance and to match names with faces. Therefore, the seat chosen as early as the first days in the semester may be the seat for the duration—perhaps for the entire year. Select carefully. Advice: choose a seat in the focus zone. Typically, your professors will spend most of their time in the center of the room, a short distance from the front row. The student who sits directly in front of the professor is more likely to engage in eye contact with the professor, remain alert throughout the entire class, hear every word spoken by the professor, hear every word spoken by students to the professor, and discern the smaller words on the blackboard—that is, never miss a beat. The focus

Does classroom participation affect your grade? Check the syllabus for each course. The practice of professors across the country is too varied to make a useful generalized statement. However, regardless of each professor's *scoring* rubrics, keep this in mind: avid, valuable class participation affects your grade in that it leads to fluency in the language of the law and provides you with more of the *practice* you need to excel in law school. This will be reflected in your grade, even if your professor doesn't actually add points to your exam score. Further, creating a good impression in class may lead to a better letter of recommendation in months or years to come—plan ahead.

zone is that triangular area with the professor's rostrum as the apex of the triangle and no further than a few rows away. The more remote you are from the professor, the more opportunities you have for distraction. In court, lawyers sit directly in front of the judge; at depositions, lawyers sit directly across from the witnesses; in their offices, lawyers sit within several feet of their clients—each of these events is based upon communication. So is class. Start practicing now.

Set up

Your classroom workspace, though limited, is your desk. In a few years, it will be your spot at the counsel table, your end of the table at the board meeting, or your podium during appellate arguments. Set up your materials and tools so they are handy. If you keep your briefs and notes on a laptop, be able to toggle back and forth; bring an extra battery (unless your school supplies a DC connection for you), and paper and pen just in case. If you use paper, have your briefs and your text open to the right spot and have several sheets of clean notepaper in front of you. Always bring an extra pen for the class—someday you will run out of ink.

Become totally involved in every class

Total involvement demands total concentration. Total involvement deepens your understanding of the complex materials you deal with daily because it forces *struggle*. You need to immerse yourself in the bending, twisting, morphing and layering of the law that occurs in nearly every class session in order come to the point where you *own* the material and can use the law to resolve legal problems. This is what you do in the professional practice of law—total involvement leads to the *passion* you will find in those who are working at their highest levels of competence.

Never chat

The time for small talk ends when the class begins. The sports scores, the market's plunge, the political upheaval, and the campus scandal all take a back seat to the law. Not only will you distract yourself, you will distract one or more other students. Even whispers are out of line in a law classroom.

Don't pass notes

Even if you need clarification on something related to what's going on in the classroom, write it in your class notes. Deal with it immediately after class. Passing a note will distract the pass*er*, the pass*ee*, several witnesses, and potentially (and worst of all) the professor.

Don't laugh

The enterprise of practicing law is a serious proposition. The law school classroom is seldom a place for frivolity. Just as the work of the courtroom, the law office, and the boardroom are serious business, so is the work of the law school classroom. Although some professors employ humor as a pedagogical tool or rhetorical device, smiles are usually the most appropriate responses to the humorous professorial comment.

As for humorous remarks made by fellow students, keep in mind that such remarks are often out of place; therefore, so is the laughter they may provoke. Also consider that what first strikes you as a humorous remark may be either a profound remark or an awkward attempt at a profound remark. In either event, laughter is an inappropriate response.

Are there exceptions to this rule? Yes, two: (1) when you are absolutely convinced the professor has said something truly funny, which she intends to provoke laughter, laugh; (2) when you are convinced a classmate has said something truly funny, which she intends to induce laughter and about which the *professor* is already laughing, laugh. However, keep in mind: if you are incorrect about the intent of either the professor or the student in exceptions (1) or (2), and you *do* laugh, you will be deservedly embarrassed, you will probably be feel obliged to apologize, and your classmates will have less respect for your prudence and discretion than they did before your audible guffaw. In law school, politeness counts. Therefore, if you believe the time to invoke one of the two exceptions has arrived, consider this: never be the first to laugh out loud.

Look at your professor

Throughout most of the class, except when you need to glance at your notes, or when you are directed to a passage in your text, or when a peer is speaking, you should follow the professor with your eyes. Why? This keeps you engaged in the class; it provides the frequent eye contact that is essential for communication (which is what the classroom experience is all about); you will always be alert and focused. Many professors agree that student/professor eye contact also makes for a better class session. Imagine teaching a group of people who are looking out the window, thumbing through their casebooks, or constantly writing. The hallmark of a great class is a spirited exchange of comments and ideas in response to questions and remarks, so eye contact between the professor and the students is an absolute essential for a lively and effective class. Do your part.

Do speak well and loudly

When you are called upon, speak to be heard. The business of most lawyers includes being heard when they speak—whether in a courtroom or in a client's office. When speaking in class, employ your "courtroom voice," a volume level which carries to the corners and walls of the classroom. Because you are engaged in a dialectic process with your classmates as well as your professor, you need to be heard by everyone in the room, including those behind you. Strive for articulate speech and strive for fluency in the language of the law. Now is the time to work on avoiding the "like, you know, I'm all, he goes, whatever, duh, and umm" expressions that brand the speaker as a non-professional. Communicate on the level of your professors and emulate their level of vocabulary, syntax, and rhetorical expertise. Law school provides the perfect training ground for exemplary oratorical skills. Even if you have a long, long way to go, keep in mind that you have a thousand days to practice.

> "You learn from your classmates by listening to them in class," writes Professor Corrine Cooper, of University of Missouri - Kansas City School of Law, "by observing their mistakes, by arguing points with them. This is not just in law school. The practice of law involves an enormous amount of this kind of give and take among lawyers, those on the same team and those across the table." Corinne Cooper, *Letter to a Young Law Student*, 35 Tulsa L.J. 275, 279 (2000).

Use your briefs as cue cards

Remember, if you have briefed the case thoroughly, the answer to every basic question the professor asks is in your brief. Even if your memory fails you, the words to get you started are right in front of you. Use each brief for its most important function—as a set of cue cards for class.

Conquer speech anxiety quickly

Some students—even those with public speaking experience—suffer from a never-before-experienced high-level speech anxiety in the law school classroom. When called upon, even to recite an elementary principle, they freeze up, panic, and become tongue-tied. The surest antidote to this phenomenon is overpreparation, rehearsal, and repeated volunteering.

- Overpreparation means preparation to the umpty-umpth degree.
- Rehearsal means practicing what will actually occur. If you suffer from speech anxiety in a particular class, visit that classroom when it is empty, and brief your cases there. Recite them out loud. Stand if you are required to stand during class recitations. If you have a study partner, hold a brief mock class in the classroom (or a similar classroom) before the actual class period and fire questions at each other.
- Volunteering brings with it several advantages. If you have prepared and rehearsed, you will be able to raise your hand for many of the questions the professor asks, and you will have the correct answers, building the professor's confidence in you. By answering questions of

> That is, know all you can know about the material you will be covering in class. If this seems too time consuming, try it for just *one* class—the one in which you have the most difficulty speaking up.

your choice, you will answer correctly more often, and you will rapidly build the self-assurance you need to respond without fear when you are called upon. Additionally, hearing your own voice and exchanging thoughts with the professor when you feel confident may make it less traumatic when the same professor singles you out for her questions.

Do not delay dealing with speech anxiety. If you put this off, you will significantly impair your development as a law student. Communication and participation in class at the highest plateaus of your personal comfort level are essential; speech anxiety can be crippling when you are practicing for a career that requires quick thinking and speaking in front of groups. If you believe your anxiety has reached a level beyond what you can deal with using self-help measures, consider asking for professional assistance to overcome this debilitating impediment.

Deal with unpreparedness

Unlike the *professional* practice of law, practice in law school is sometimes forgiving. If the day comes that you are unprepared—that is, you have not read and briefed the required material prior to class—your best bet is usually a proactive notification to your professor. Most professors prefer an acknowledgement of unpreparedness prior to class; they will mark your name on the seating chart, pass you over when calling on students, and not waste any class time or provide you undue embarrassment. Be forewarned that repeated instances of unpreparedness are frowned upon, and know that many professors consider an unprepared student (whether disclosed prior to class or discovered during class) as an absent student. Never attempt to fool your professor into thinking you are prepared when you are not. These men and women are experts; they know. So do most of your classmates. Neither your professors nor your peers will appreciate your wasting their time.

Being unprepared and not knowing the answer to a professor's question are different. When you *are* prepared, but you don't know the answer, attempt to answer if you have a clue—many professors will work with students and draw answers from them that the students themselves didn't realize they were capable of providing. If you truly can't come up with anything satisfactory, remember these glorious words, "anonymous grading on exams," and admit that you haven't a clue.

Toughen up

If you suffer through a class in which a professor relentlessly returns to you for answers to questions beyond your ken, don't let that get you down. The professional practice of law is fraught with instances of embarrassment, frustration, and intellectual challenges. So is the practice of law in law school. On the other hand, if you repeatedly find that you are "lost" in class—seek help. This is the time to turn to your professors and your law school's academic support professionals, whose expertise your tuition dollars have purchased. Delay can be devastating.

Lawyers Take Notes

During trials, depositions, appellate hearings, client interviews, witness interviews, telephone conversations, firm meetings, continuing education classes—lawyers take notes. These notes are more or less valuable, depending upon how closely they meet the lawyer's objective. That goal is usually to create a personal record of spoken words for later reference. While writing notes, the lawyer cannot afford to lose track of what is being said (orally or non-verbally) by the speaker—any given word, phrase, glance, or smile may be packed with more meaning than what is being committed to paper at that moment. Superior effective note-taking, as a lawyer, takes considerable practice. Lawyers are expert note-takers.

Successful Law Students Become Expert Note Takers

Law students' primary goal in taking notes in class is precisely the same as the lawyers' goal: to create a personal record for later reference. In addition, law students and lawyers have *other* reasons for note-taking, including:

- *Vigilance.* Taking notes keeps you focused.
- *Recall.* During class you discover what you forgot to read, what you need to look up, and questions you need answered. Noting these items keeps them from evaporating into the atmosphere.
- *Retention.* Writing notes, then *working with them soon thereafter*, dramatically increases the incidence of retention of the material.
- *Exam preparation.* The richest source of fundamental information for course summary preparation will be your class notes.

Do these match your objectives? If they are even close, the following method of note-taking will be ideal for you.

Nuts & Bolts: Taking Notes in Law School
The POINTSystem of Note-Taking

Students employ various note-taking strategies in law school—some are very effective, many less so. Consider using the Powerful Organized Integrated Note-Taking System (the POINTSystem) set out below. If you decide to use a laptop for note-taking, the POINTSystem is easily adaptable. Follow these steps:

- *Gather essential materials.* For each course, use a separate, sturdy, three-ring binder, with plastic end panels (those pieces of hard plastic designed to keep papers from curling), and tabbed dividers (to separate syllabus, handouts, briefs, class notes, and reading notes). Purchase a quality 3-hole punch and a set of highlighters. Find "law-ruled" paper. Make sure to bring lots of paper to each class.

- *Organize and label each page.* Apply the following information to each note page: course name, date, page number. This information is essential for later referencing, when you use your notes to compile course summaries.

- *Record class notes.* Write your notes on the right side of the red margin line, with plenty of white space. Write neatly. Use abbreviations as much as possible.

- *Write only the essentials.* What occurs in class is a "process." You can't adequately record a "process" in class notes. What you need to write down, to accomplish the four objectives, turns out to be *not very much.* Therefore, the first rule of what to write is this: *not* everything. On a more positive note, here's what you *should* write in your notes:

  - *Magic words.* You are learning the language of the law. You will recognize that the professor emphasizes certain words and phrases by repetition, spelling them, writing them on the board, or flat out telling you they are important to know.

  - *Everything written on the board.* Some professors write nothing on the board. Some cover it. Whatever is written there is being *repeated* (emphasized) in that the professor presents it to you orally *and* in writing.

  - *Every flow chart or diagram drawn on board.* Flow charts and diagrams are thinking "maps." The professor is demonstrating hierarchies of principles, relationships of parties, development of doctrines, chronological relativity, or some other relationship capable of spatial representation. She wants you to comprehend it as drawn.

  - *All hypotheticals.* Hypothetical narratives are the meat and potatoes of law classes, *and* you will have to respond to them on your examinations. When your professor provides hypotheticals during class, she is offering you superb practice material (for exam-answering practice) and insight into how she thinks (vis-à-vis generation of exam questions), and, quite possibly, a preview of an actual exam question.

  - *Articulation (by your professor) of rules, definitions, tests, standards, and exceptions.* Your textbook and commercial outlines are jam-packed with these. But your professor tells you very clearly *which* of them she wants you to know, *and* she tells you the precise words she will recognize as a perfectly articulate expression of each of them.

> You may find some white paper and pale green (easy on the eyes) "law-ruled" paper at your bookstore. "Law-ruled" notepaper has the red margin drawn several inches from the left side of the page, providing a very useful bi-columnar setup.

> This organization and labeling is equally important after bar admission, for cross-referencing during meetings, trials, and other situations during which quick information retrieval is essential.

> "First, don't write down everything the professor and other students say. Remember: this is not college. You are not required to regurgitate, word for word, the professor's brilliant speeches. You are required to use the information to solve new problems." Stropus & Taylor, 42.

- *Analytical tips offered by your professor.* The most important part of any law school examination answer is the *analysis* part. When your professor says, "Here's how you analyze a 'proximate cause' issue," she is telling you precisely how she expects you to approach a similar issue on her examination.

- *Student comments, if intriguing or if praised by the professor (include student's name).* Most student comments and inquiries raised in class will have some value—but most of that value lies in their *process* value, rather than their *content* value. Every once in a while, your professor may say, "Did everyone hear that? Say it again, Mr. Slocum, so we all hear it." Anytime you are so tipped off, write down what Mr. Slocum says, even if you don't understand its import at the time. That is why you write his name by the comment—that afternoon or six weeks down the road, if it turns out to be important, you will know whom to ask for an explanation.

> The value of many student comments in class is not their inherent substantive value, but the value they provide in moving the discussion along.

- *Policy.* Professors love policy. You will want to show them *you* love it, too. You are in law school to study jurisprudence, the philosophy of the law. Philosophy includes investigation into underlying theories and principles. In the field of law, these are (or relate to) "policy." Policies, in this sense, relate to standards of, or assumptions about, morality, economics, social considerations, administrative economy and efficiency, ecological concerns, political necessities—and on and on—there's a policy issue pertaining to just about every aspect of the law. Law professors point these policies out all semester long—they expect you to be able to analyze problems with policy considerations in mind. You need to know the policies to understand what drives the analyses.

- *Constitutional aspects.* The United States Constitution is "the law of the land." Any time a professor explains that a law has its basis, or its *raison d'être*, in a constitutional provision, she wants you to remember that.

- *Distinctions, differences, and similarities to other cases, laws, and statutes.* The study (and use) of law is a study in distinctions, differences, and similarities. The arguments you will learn to construct will be based on categorizations, comparisons, and analogies. Thus, when your professor points out such things in class, write them down.

The other types of notes to make during class are related to the briefs you have in front of you as the class considers the cases. These notes are adjustments to your brief. Make these adjustments *directly on your case briefs*. What adjustments? From time to time, you will notice that you misunderstood some aspect of the case and reflected this misinterpretation in your brief, so change it. Add the extra sub-issue; correctly restate the rule; insert that salient fact; revise that cogent rationale—but do it *on the brief*. Why? So that when you return to the brief as a synopsis of the essentials of the case (as you will during the course summarizing activity you will embark upon later), you do not have to fumble through notes looking for the lost fact—it will be right where it's supposed to be. As soon as you leave class, you should attend to the third component of assessment-targeted study—transformation of your notes.

Component 3
Transform Your Notes

Practicing Lawyers Transform Their Notes

Something had gone terribly wrong during the construction process. Everyone around the table acknowledged the depth of the problem ... but no one wanted to claim responsibility for arriving at this point.

Earlier in the week, Francis Moyal had retained Kristine Perry as the attorney he would rely upon to negotiate a way out of the situation or to defend him and his company, Environmental Engineering Company, in federal court, should it come to that. The meeting this morning—scheduled to last all day—was to acquaint Ms. Perry with the entire project and how it went awry. She had asked Francis for the opportunity to meet all the "players" and to hear their variety of perspectives. This is why the construction manager, field foremen, engineering superintendent, and the equipment specialist gathered around the Holiday Inn conference room table at 6:00 a.m.

The table was covered with files containing correspondence, specifications, subcontracts, invoices, and memoranda of every description—tubes of rolled-up blueprints occupied nearly half the table—there must have been 200 of them.

"How," Kristine thought silently to herself, "am I going to learn all about the construction of a 50,000 kilowatt hydroelectric generating plant in a day?" As quickly as the thought formed in her mind, so did the answer: "Listen carefully, ask questions, write down everything that seems important"—just as she had learned to do in law school, just as she did every day as she interviewed clients and witnesses.

By 4:00 p.m., the group was breaking up—several of the men announced their intention to head across the street to the River Glen Tavern to have a couple of beers—they politely invited EEC's new lawyer. Just as politely, Kris declined, then headed straight to her hotel room, for the day's work was not yet over. She knew she had to spend an hour or two alone, transforming the day's notes into a product that would become the foundation of her familiarization with the facts and law involved in this complex struggle between the contractor and the consortium of energy production companies who hired EEC to build the facility.

The process of note transformation was something she had learned in law school ... accumulating the raw data, then sorting and categorizing it according to topic, function, source, action, and inquiry.

Kris knew that by actively processing the fresh raw data, she would fix the important points in her mind, clarify some of those matters that had seemed fuzzy during the meeting, and develop a long list of specific questions that she would be asking Francis Moyal the next morning. The process would also yield a discrete series of legal questions she would be able to answer later that evening, when she went online to begin her legal research. By the time of Kris's early morning meeting with Francis, not only would she have a good grip on the facts of the case, but she would have visited several online sources for some in-depth reading to fill in the gaps—definitions of construction terms, for example. She would have developed a degree of fluency in the language of hydro-electric plant construction, and the laws that govern it. Francis would know he had hired the right lawyer.

When lawyers jot essential words and phrases, often in makeshift shorthand, on those yellow legal pads, they know that these notes need to be transformed into something more permanent as soon as possible. They know that stale, sketchy notes are useless notes. Notes made during meetings, phone conversations, depositions, hearings, and trials need to be *transformed* into something more substantial if they are going to be useful—and this transformation must occur as soon as possible. Lawyers transform their notes.

Start Practicing Now: Transform Your Notes

Even the best of notes include evanescent references, abbreviations that make sense when written, and bits and pieces of quotations, thoughts, and analytical stratagems that make perfect sense in the context of the classroom discussion, then little or no sense a week later.

As much as 80 percent of what was "learned" in a classroom will be forgotten within a few hours—taking notes is a method to preserve class content and an essential ingredient in the recipe to prevent total disappearance of that content from your mind. However, notes left untouched are notes not worth taking.

Notes, once written, remain *passive*. Effective learning is *active*. Give your notes *power*: immediately transform them from passive entries in your notebook or computer to action-provoking, engaging catalysts for learning. Put your raw data to work.

Immediate transformation of your class notes from raw data to categorized information, memory cues, specific inquiries, and basic materials for your personal course summaries will make your note taking worthwhile.

Your class notes *should* be incomplete and need immediate (after-class) transformation. Acting as a scrivener during class—writing down everything—interferes with active learning. Write what you need and immediately attend to the transformation *after* the active learning session ends.

Nuts and Bolts: Transforming Class Notes

The POINT System continues after the class period ends. Once you have taken the notes in the classroom and the *activity* of taking notes has served its purpose of keeping you alert and focused, you need to begin your transformation of the notes into something of considerable value *long after* the class period. Notes remain useless artifacts until completed, transformed, and employed.

Step One—Complete the notes

To complete the notes, fill in the "note holes." Note holes are the blanks in your notes. Very early in the semester, reach an agreement with a student—preferably a good note-taker who sits near you. The terms of the note-taking agreement should be that you will meet immediately after class, preferably before you leave the classroom, for under 60 seconds, to ask each other, "What goes here?"

> Note holes like this:
> "First degree murder is deliberate, _____, and premeditated."

Step Two—Begin to transform the notes

Take your notes from raw materials to useful products. As soon as possible after class—within minutes if you have a break—highlight and summarize your notes. To *highlight*, use a highlighter, marking only those words and phrases you believe to be the outstanding "highlights" of the class. With the perspective you have at the *end* of the class, you are in a much better position to make this determination than you were *during* the class—and the information is still fresh in your mind, so its significance remains apparent. Then *summarize* or *headline* the notes by neatly writing or printing the *topic* word or phrase, or a brief descriptor, on the left side of the red margin line.

> "It is imperative that you review your notes the same day as class, while the material is fresh in your mind."
> Stropus & Taylor, 51.

Within several hours, complete the transformation of your notes by recasting them—mold them into what will be most useful for you in terms of achieving your objective.

As your notebook (binder) is open, the page on the right side will include the notes taken in class and the summary/headline words added after class. The page on the *left* side—that is, the *back* side of the classroom notes—is blank. Fill that. What goes there? Generate three categories of information:

> *These* are the pages over which students toil and sweat. Accordingly, the learning experts at Landmark College (Putney, Vermont) have aptly nicknamed these "sweat pages."

- *Summary of what you covered in class.* Succinctly state the principles, rules and exceptions discussed in class. Include every "term of art" or word or phrase with a special definition.
- *Visuals.* Whether by way of cartoons, stick figures, diagrams or mini flow charts, try to express the principles with visuals, if you have the talent.
- *Questions.* Shortly after class, develop questions of three types:
    - What remains unclear?
    - How does this information relate to other material in *this* course, material in *another* course, and/or personal experience?
    - How might this appear on an exam?

At that point, your notes have been "transformed"—the next step is to begin employing them. These notes will constitute the primary source material for your course summary. But before you get to that stage, you need to answer the questions you wrote on the "sweat page."

Step Three—Answer the questions

The first set of questions should send you to your casebook, hornbook, or commercial course summary. If you have read and briefed the material, engaged actively in the class, and still cannot figure out what the professor meant when she used the word "battery," it is time to look it up and write it down. The questions you have written—simple or profound—should be answered before the next class period. If you are unable to find answers by turning to other written sources, ask your professor. Most professors are pleased to respond to such questions during office hours or via email. Some begin classes with inquiries, "Before we move along, does anyone have any questions from the last class?" Jump in.

The second set of questions, about how the information covered in class relates to other information stored in your bank of knowledge or experience, can be answered by careful reflection and, at times, turning the pages of a book from another class.

The third set of questions ("How might this appear on an exam?") does not mean you need to write examination questions. Rather, professors will often let students know where the "tension" in a given topical area lies. In this sense, *tension* is related to the bipolar viewpoints, perspectives, or objectives associated with a concept. For example, the death penalty is viewed by those who believe criminal sanctions are for the purpose of *punishing* criminals one way and by those who believe criminal sanctions are for the purpose of *deterring* criminals another way. Often, arguments advanced by those espousing two such viewpoints will tug in opposite directions. Professors expect students to be

According to UNLV's Professor Pavel Wonsowicz, hornbooks and commercial study aids should be your last resort. "The answer," he explains, "is nearly always in the casebook." He suggests that when the going gets tough, students learn deepest when they struggle for the answer rather than taking the shortcuts offered by commercial study aids.

When sending e-mail to your professor, use the spellchecker and grammar checker on your computer. Read your message aloud, to make sure it is written at your highest level of composition competence. Soon you will be sending e-mail to judges, law partners, and clients. Practice law now.

An *ambiguous* word is susceptible to more than one meaning. For example, if an essential element in the proof of a contract case is "disclosure" of the identity of one of the parties to the contract by that party's agent, how much identification constitutes "disclosure" would be a potential area of ambiguity. If a legal principle could result in different outcomes depending upon the interpretation of different courts, perhaps the principle is *uncertain*. An apparently benign doctrine may be *vulnerable* if, for example, its application in a particular circumstance may be unconstitutionally discriminatory.

aware of these *tensions* and to be able to adeptly manifest that awareness in exam answers. So, the answer to "How might this appear on an exam?" should point to the area of tension, ambiguity, uncertainty, or vulnerability of a doctrine or concept discussed in class. At this point in your notes (on the "sweat page") make sure to mention this potentially discussible area and to indicate potential resolutions.

How long should all this take? After each class, the process of putting your notes in shape for later use should take just a few minutes. Consider these as example times:

- Note hole filling—1 minute.
- Highlighting and summarizing—2 minutes.
- Sweat page writing—4 minutes.
- Answering questions you write on the sweat page—3 minutes (or much longer if you have many in-depth questions).

Perform this 10-minute (or more) transformational exercise after each class. Your notes will become your best resource for production of your course summaries.

Component 4
Prepare Course Summaries

Practicing Lawyers Prepare Trial Books

"And what," the defendant's attorney asked slowly and precisely, with a sideward glance at the jury box, "was going through your mind when you signed that contract, Mr. Parillo?"

Ellen Hoover, representing the plaintiff, an elderly widower who sat beside her, shot up from her seat at the counsel table before Parillo could formulate an answer and practically shouted, "Objection, Your Honor."

"On what grounds?" inquired the silver-haired judge presiding over the jury trial.

"Your Honor, the secret intent of the witness at the time of the creation of the contract is irrelevant. The objective manifestation of what he intended is all that this court—and this jury—should be concerned with."

After a moment, the judge turned to the lawyer who had asked the question, and asked, "Well, Mr. Spillane, what do you have to say about that? I believe counsel is correct. How is Mr. Parillo's intent relevant to the question of the contract's validity?"

"Respectfully, Your Honor," Mitch Spillane responded, "I agree that Mr. Parillo's intent is irrelevant to the issue of validity of the contract—however, it is very important as to the question of whether he engaged in the fraud of which he is accused by Ms. Hoover's client."

"Please approach the bench, counsel."

As the two lawyers walked the few steps to the side of the judge's bench for a conference outside of the earshot of the jurors, Ellen paused momentarily to grab a grey three-ring binder.

Mitch Spillane, using a barely audible near whisper, immediately explained to the attentive judge that his client had never intended to mislead the plaintiff, and that the line of questioning he intended to pursue—concerning the state of mind of his client—was essential to his defense.

"Essential, no doubt, Your Honor, but unavailable." Ellen unsnapped a document from the three-ring binder she carried, and handed it to the judge. "Your Honor, when Mr. Spillane and his client responded to our 'Request For Admissions' last July, as Your Honor will note at line 20, they took that issue out of the case by admitting that the representations made in the first few words of the contract were false and 'known to be false' by Mr. Parillo."

"Further, Your Honor," Ellen continued, "Under Mercy Hospital v. Slocum, *decided only last week by our Supreme Court, just such an inquiry was held to be irrelevant in a case practically identical to ours." As she spoke these words, she handed the judge and Mr. Spillane copies of the* Mercy Hospital *case, which she deftly produced from the pocket section of the same binder.*

After quickly studying the two papers before him, Judge Willoughby announced aloud, "Objection sustained. Move on to other matters, Mr. Spillane."

Replacing the grey binder next to the other two identical binders on the counsel table, Ellen nodded ever-so-slightly to Jim Lasko, her trial assistant. He knew that nod. It meant, "Thanks for keeping my Trial Book up to date, Jim—that just got us out of a real pickle."

> Although the trial book becomes a powerful reference tool for the trial itself, much of its strategic content is passé by the time of trial; however, quick access at trial to pleadings, discovery materials, and a multiplicity of documentary references and reminders remains essential.

Trial books, "device(s) most experienced trial lawyers use in some form to help organize materials and thoughts,"[12] are summarized versions of every significant aspect of the case a lawyer brings to trial. "The [trial] notebook," explain attorneys Paul I. Weiner and Charles C. Warner, "is a summary or outline of the trial."[13]

Often, as in the above vignette, parts of actual pleadings and briefs or copies of pertinent precedential cases supplement the summaries. Trial books are usually organized according to issues to be addressed at trial, by witnesses expected to testify, by pleadings, and by important documents to be introduced as evidence. By creating the trial book throughout the weeks or months of preparation for the actual trial, the lawyer builds, streamlines, edits, and often refashions her perception (and ultimately her presentation) of the case. By supplementing, revising and reorganizing her trial book, she cements every issue, sub-issue, and twist into her consciousness.

Start Practicing Now: Prepare Course Summaries

> The word "production" derives from the Latin *producere*, to bring forth. The activity of producing a course summary *brings forth* a rich, deep, useful comprehension of each subject.

The law school analogue to the litigator's trial book is the course summary. Just as production of a trial book is essential to total mastery of the matter under litigation, production of a course summary should aim at but one objective: mastery of a subject. During your first year of law school, you will discover the challenge of transforming what seems to be "passive" education into intellectually "active" education. Although your professors will often promote out-of-class intellectual engagement of the substantive material, they do not detail how it is to be done. This is how: create a course summary.

Creation of your course summary is the next essential step in subject mastery. Creation of the course summary provides the horsepower that drives your spaced-study of the course and the navigation to keep your study going in the right directions. The process of summary production dramatically elevates the likelihood of your learning each subject deeply, accurately, strategically, schematically, and course-specifically.

Deeply. Superficial understanding of a topic within a course—or of the entire course—inevitably leads to student confusion. Even if the student does not recognize the confusion, be assured that the professor will as she reads the exam answers. Go deep.

Accurately. The practice of law demands and rewards accuracy. So also, professors reward accurate, complete definitions of fundamental legal terms, precise statements of basic legal doctrines, and correct application of underlying policies and principles.

Strategically. A course summary designed to facilitate learning and customized to interweave chronologically, topically, and functionally with the other essential components of assessment-targeted study is a *strategic* summary of the course. Use of the words "strategy" infers an objective. Here, the objective is clear: the ability to consistently demonstrate total mastery of a topical area of the law, by fluently demonstrating your capability to analyze facts and present cogent written analytical arguments and explanations. Achievement of this objective will earn you the highest grade you are capable of earning. Just as importantly, the practice of designing, undertaking, and tenaciously following through with your strategy will prepare you for the professional practice of law.

Schematically. You will encounter many doctrines, theories, principles, policies, statutes, rules and definitions during the first few months of law school. The need to "schematize" them, to form them into a system of relationships, is of paramount importance. These systematized relationships, or "knowledge structures," allow for "cognitive economy,"[14] and efficiency of comprehension. Once you know where everything "fits" in the scheme of things, you will truly be able to understand it. Without that knowledge, you will have nothing but a hodge-podge of disconnected facts and legal principles.

Course-specifically. With rare exception (almost always announced by the professor) law school exams are written to test students' knowledge and skills within a defined universe of topics. For example, you may notice that your Contracts casebook or commercial study aid includes dozens of topics, each with its own array of subdivided com-

---

Perhaps unsurprisingly, "passive" finds its root in the Latin word *passus*, "suffering."

Superficial understanding— note the oxymoron.

Our English word "strategy" comes from the combination of the Greek words *stratos* (army) and *agein* (to lead), which generated the Latin word *strategema*, meaning "the act of a general." What a powerful metaphor that word implies for the study —and the *practice*—of law.

The word "schema" derives from the Greek *skhema*, meaning "form."

ponents, corollaries, and exceptions. Nevertheless, your professor will likely only cover the topics she considers to be the most fundamental, interesting, or within her special scope of superior academic interest and expertise. Many professors manifest distinct preferences for heavy emphasis on the relation of each doctrinal point to a larger principle—economic, moral, philosophical, or constitutional. Others are more insistent on intense analysis of facts, and the related logical operations of analogy, categorization, and distinction. Without exception, law professors manifest their preferences (that is, their preferences for what you should be writing in your exam answers) during class and during one-to-one office conferences. A course-specific course summary matches the content, expectations, and points-of-view of the course as designed and delivered by the professor (read "exam grader"—get the point?).

Who should create your course summary?

You. Not BarBri. Not Gilberts. Not Emanuel. Not a second or third-year law student friend. Not Professor Glannon. You. Many high-level, well-recognized commercial study aids are very helpful to provide structure, comparisons, augmentations, precise definitions, and formatting ideas for your own course summary. None of them, or any combination of them, can take the place of your personal summary. Why? Simply because the *practice* is in the construction and development of the product. When you spend the time and mental energy to produce your own course summary, you are *actively* learning. Trial attorneys develop their own trial notebooks for the same reason—they *actively* learn the subject matter.

What is a course summary?

A course summary is an abstract and synthesis of the course as taught by the professor, as augmented and explained by outside resources, and as understood by the student.

Law students (and many professors) refer to course summaries as "outlines." The term is misleading. Somewhere between fourth and tenth grade, you probably learned how to "outline." The outline format you learned probably consisted of words, phrases, or entire sentences—topics, subtopics, and sub-subtopics—listed in a series following Roman numerals, upper case letters, and parenthesized Arabic numerals, much like this:

Professors Fischl & Paul write, "Listen carefully to every word your professor says about what she wants in an exam and try to provide it." Richard Michael Fischl & Jeremy Paul, *Getting to Maybe: How to Excel on Law School Exams*, 242 (Carolina Academic Press 1999).

BarBri is a commercial bar exam preparation company that produces in-depth summaries of every course tested by bar examiners across the country; *Gilberts Outlines* are commercial study aids; the Emanuel company publishes a plethora of study aids; Professor Glannon is the author of helpful summaries of some first-year subjects. None of these products should take the place of the course summaries *you* produce.

"The process of taking all the individual pieces (e.g., rules from cases) and connecting them is called *synthesis*. It is the most vital skill to master to do well on exams and become a successful lawyer. Stropus & Taylor, 53.

I. Negligence
- A. Duty
- B. Breach of Duty
    1. Objective Standard
    2. Subjective Standard
- C. Causation
    1. Actual Causation
    2. Proximate Cause
- D. Damages
- E. Defenses
    1. Self-defense
    2. Defense of Others
    3. Defense of Property
    4. Necessity
        - (a) Public Necessity
        - (b) Private Necessity

> The "negligence" outline in the text is woefully incomplete and set forth only as a stylistic example.

Some law students produce "outlines" which look like the foregoing and believe they have "outlined" the course. Perhaps they have. However, outlines like that provide little or no help in achieving the objectives of fluency in the language of the law, preparation for the professional practice of law, obtaining grades reflective of your personal best efforts, and passing the bar exam on the first sitting. The "outline" may provide an organized, schematically categorized skeletal layout for the summary of your course—the product *you* should create is a *course summary*. Your course summary should be *your book* on the subject, as learned from *your* professor. No other summary will do. You need to create it from scratch, and it needs to be extremely course/professor specific.

> Note the vast differences between an "outline" (such as the "negligence" example above) and a *course summary* as described in this section.

Most law students wrote some form of "senior thesis" or "capstone paper" for a course or major field of undergraduate or graduate study. Those who did recognize that by the time they completed their work, they believed they had mastered the topic. By researching, writing, editing, revising, and supplementing their thesis paper over several weeks, they became so familiar with—*and fluent in the language of*—the topic; they could have delivered a lecture, or held their own in a high-level discussion, probably without notes. Did you have this experience? If so, you probably felt rather conversant in the jargon of that field and in tune with the denotative and connotative meanings of the terms of art employed by professionals or scholars in that field of study. So, too, first-year law students who are the authors of their own custom-designed, strategic, course-specific texts on each subject attain a high level of mastery of each subject. So, too, *you*—as a first-year law student—should earn this justifiable self-confidence in the fields of Torts, Contracts, Civil Procedure, and every other law school course you intend to excel in. To get there, you need to produce an in-depth written product: your personal course summary.

When should you create your course summaries?

In most first-year, first-semester courses, the ideal time to begin composing a summary is about the fourth week of class. By that time, you will have caught on to the routine of reading and briefing (class preparation), class attendance, and note-taking (participation and follow-up). Your schedule should compress a bit as you become more agile at these components, allowing for some time each week to devote to summarizing each of your courses. By week four, you will also have assembled a suitable mass of material to organize, synthesize, and supplement. In the semesters that follow, you will be able to commence summarizing earlier in the semester since you will already have sufficient practice at the first three components of the CATS.

Once you begin your summary in each subject, commit to revising, supplementing, and extending each summary weekly, while the new material is still fresh in your memory. Your objective is to complete each summary long before reading week.

Nuts and Bolts: Preparing Course Summaries

How do you create your course summary? To write a course summary, follow these ten steps (detailed below):

1. Gather essential materials.
2. Generally organize subject matter.
3. Collect fundamental rules and divide rules into elements.
4. Identify alternative and minority rules.
5. Illustrate each point.
6. Include policy rationale.
7. Add cases as examples.
8. Format to manifest hierarchical alignment.
9. Revise as necessary.
10. Verify completeness and usefulness.

Step One—Gather essential materials

After establishing your quality study environment (see supplement)—as distraction-free as a judge's chambers—assemble on your desk:

- Your casebook and any required or suggested (by your professor) course supplements you own.

- Your fully annotated transformed class notes.
- Your briefs, including all revisions.
- Your favorite commercial study aid (if any).

If your notes or briefs are stored on your computer, consider printing them to avoid switching from screen to screen.

Step Two—Generally organize subject matter

This is the beginning step of actual drafting—this is where you begin to perform the first stages of lawyerly writing: categorization.

Categories are ubiquitous and inescapable in the use of [the] mind. Nobody can do without them—not lawyers or judges, Hottentot farmers or school children... Categories are the badges of our sociopolitical allegiances, the tools of our mental life, the organizers of our perception.[15]

Jeremy Paul, Professor of Law at the University of Connecticut and Michael Fischl, Professor of Law at University of Miami, write, "Virtually every lawyer will agree that the law uses categories extensively.... [T]he law can group into broad categories and establish rules covering each."[16] For example specific and distinctly different rules apply to determine the legal rights of people who incur injuries while on someone else's premises, according to whether they are categorized as social friends, guests with business purposes in mind, unauthorized entrants, children, or adults. Likewise, the liability of the owner of the premises to an injured person may depend on which category she falls into: one who knew of the injury-causing problem, one who did not know but *should have* known, one who is conducting ultrahazardous activities on her land, and so on.

"To put something in a category is to assign it a meaning, to place it in a particular context of ideas." Amsterdam & Bruner, 28.

Lawyers think, argue, and write in terms of categories. "Thinking like a lawyer," Professor Daniel Kleinberger of William Mitchell College of Law points out, "includes ... analyzing situations by defining categories of behavior and then attaching consequences to those categories." This, he explains, is a fundamental way "in which lawyers understand the world."[17] Professors Fischl and Paul insist that "You can't begin to see why law school exams generate so many hard problems until you grasp the importance of categories to legal disputes."[18] Since this is the case, begin your course summary of each subject by categorizing. The first stage of categorizing is organization under topical headings.

You will find the general substantive headings you need in several places. Start with your professor's syllabus. Either she has divided the semester into chunks designated by topical references, or she has set out specific casebook reading assignments (or both). Thus, the major summary headings are supplied directly by the syllabus or indirectly through the casebook's table of contents and chapter headings. Secondary level headings for your summary—in other words, subcategories, subtopics, or subdivisions of the main (more general) classifications—are evident from the same sources (syllabi and tables of contents) and two other sources: your class notes and your commercial study aids. Although many students confidently craft superb summaries without the assistance of a commercial study aid, others find them to be quite helpful. By the end of your first month of law school, you will have been exposed to several different commercial resources for each course. Peruse several at your campus bookstore, in the office of your academic support staff, in the school library, or borrow some from friends. Read the descriptions of several study aids in the special supplement in this book. Decide for yourself which, if any, seem to be helpful in each subject—then use no more than one per subject.

Step Three—Collect fundamental rules and divide rules into elements

Write the legal rules directly associated with each topical heading (including all the secondary level headings in your summary). You will find these rules in a variety of places. Search for them in this order:

First—search your class notes. If your professor has articulated a rule of law and you captured it verbatim in your notes, use that expression of the rule.

Second—search your revised briefs. Your case briefs, as augmented during class, should include precise, articulate statements of the principles of law designated by the topical headings in your course summary. Be aware that many court opinions are included in casebooks because their decisions are anomalous, providing superb catalysts for classroom discussion. Therefore, not every case's "holding" or statement of a legal principle is generally accepted—you should be able to determine which cases fall into this class by the notes following such cases in your text and by the comments of your professor during class.

Third—search the commercial study aid you have selected. But be *very* selective as to what you extract from commercial study aids. Although most of the best-selling study aids set forth concise, accurate statements of the fundamental principles of the law, they may deviate from the emphasis your professor prefers. Therefore, the most serious problem is not really that you risk being *under*informed, but rather, you face a substantial risk of information overload. Because of their universal use and acceptance by students, publishers of commercial study aids strive for inclusiveness, not wanting to be accused of leaving out something significant. However, since *your* professor's view of what is significant differs markedly from other professors' views—and since some courses are more extensive (in duration, coverage and credit) at some schools than at others—you can be quite confident that most commercial resources will include masses of information not covered in your class, not mentioned by your professor, and not included in your assigned casebook reading. In short, the rules, principles, distinctions, classifications, definitions, exceptions, statutory deviations, minority rules, model codes, case references, and illustrations you will encounter in commercial study aids generally should not be used to *expand* your course summary. Stick primarily to information your professor and your casebook impart—use the rules as set forth in the commercial summaries, hornbooks, nutshells, and flashcards only as material to fill in gaps in your notes.

Complete step three by dividing each rule into its elemental parts. For example, assume that a "rule" in the field of contracts is that an "offer" (an essential element of many legally enforceable contracts) must "create a reasonable expectation" in the mind of the other party ("offeree") that the offeror is willing to enter into a contract on the basis of the terms offered. You will discover that in deciding whether a communication creates this reasonable expectation, you will need to address three questions: (1) Was there an expression of a promise, undertaking, or commitment to enter into a contract? (2) Were the essential terms certain and definite? (3) Was there a communication of (1) and (2) to the offeree? In your Contracts course summary, after stating the elemental rule relating to the necessity of an offer, you should include as subdivisions: (1) Promise, undertaking, or commitment, (2) Definite and certain terms, and (3) Communication.

> This illustration is merely an example. If your professor employs a different strategic analysis, that, of course, takes precedence over this paragraph.

Each of these subdivisions should be further divided, including applicable definitions and legal standards. This process of narrowing, parsing, and categorizing, should be mentally taxing, intellectually challenging, and often frustrating. Again, welcome to the practice of law, where such taxes, challenges, and frustrations constitute the very fabric of most lawyers' daily professional practice.

Each "rule" related to each element in this hierarchical structuring and organizational effort must be stated in the precise terms your professor employs and/or in the words of the alternative and supportive authoritative sources you have chosen. For a dozen years, beginning in elementary school, you have heard this exhortation from teacher after teacher: "Put it in your own words." Putting legal principles, maxims, rules, exceptions, terms, and definitions into your own words will almost assure you of lower (than you deserve) grades in law school and less success in the professional practice. From your first days of law school, you should practice using the words of others. In the practice of law, you

> Although the language of the law includes a precise vocabulary, command of the vocabulary alone does not amount to *fluency*. The capability to deftly weave these words and expressions together to form cogent and persuasive written discourse is the hallmark of sound legal writing.

will discover that it is the creative and artful employment, deployment and critical analysis of the words of others that is the bread and butter of legal reasoning and writing. The application of enduring principles, heretofore crafted and developed with care and precision by earlier generations of jurists, scholars, and legislators to the unique facts and circumstances of individual cases is the essence of legal writing. The daily work of the lawyer centers on the operation of facts, logic, and persuasive rhetoric with and upon the words and expressions that constitute the law.

Use your own words to persuade your audience (whether that is a law professor today or a jury or judge tomorrow), but never, never put the *law* "in your own words."

Step Four—Identify alternative and minority rules

Scour your class notes and authoritative resources for principles, rules, and statutes that may be (or have been) used to reach results other than those dictated by the primary rules. Alternative rules are those that the court may use in cases which (even ever-so-slightly) deviate from the standard. For example, you will discover that the rules which prescribe the degree of duty to provide a safe environment for guests is different for an innkeeper than for a grocery store owner, different for a taxi driver than for the fellow who rents bicycles at the park. Judges who decide cases, lawyers who argue cases, and students who write exam answers search for alternatives as they write. Professors who grade examinations reward students who recognize "forks in the law" or "forks in the facts" arising from ambiguities in the facts, statutes or precedential court decisions, or from variations in local customs or changes in underlying policy considerations, and who resolve these legal conundra by applying alternative standards or rules.

> This concept of recognizing and addressing "forks" in law and fact is thoroughly discussed by professors Fischl & Paul in chapters 2 through 7 of *Getting to Maybe*.

Minority rules are significant variations in the law that are employed by fewer than half the states. Most law professors expect students to recognize that not all jurisdictions follow the same laws. Since law exams often do not provide clues as to whether the fictional hypothetical situations detailed in the question occur in states applying the majority or minority rules, savvy students will point out the possible disparate results under each.

Step Five—illustrate each point

"To illustrate" is to clarify by use of examples, comparisons, or explanations. Again, your most helpful source for illustrative material should be your class notes, which should include hypothetical examples of the laws "in action," as provided by your professor during class. Law professors are master crafters of illustrative, enlightening hypotheticals.

Most of your classes will be liberally peppered with these fictional stories, many of which "push the envelope" of logic and credulity, forcing students to explore the extreme boundaries of common sense, social policy, morality, and justice. Inclusion of significant hypotheticals in your summary can strengthen your understanding and reinforce your recollection.

To "illustrate" can also mean to supplement your text with explanatory pictures and diagrams. Visual learners should consider augmenting their writing with diagrams, schematics, and even stick-figure cartoons. The power of visual aids to fortify recollection is well-documented and can be an invaluable tool for many students. Some students benefit from colorizing their summaries. For example, you might use your highlighter to color all fundamental rules green and all exceptions yellow.

> It is essential to *explain* the law in your course summary—so that your summary is not merely a simple reflection of a series of rules, laws, and definitions that have little or no meaning to *you*, the author, and exclusive audience of the course summary. This *explanation* of the law *should* be in your own words (contrast this with the advice under step three, above).

Step Six—Include policy rationale

Learning law without learning policy is like learning chess moves without learning why or how to make the moves. Most every rule of law lawyers encounter emanates from a legislative or judicial intent to promote or preserve an economic, commercial, moral, utilitarian, retributive, national security, or social policy designed to "insure domestic tranquility, provide for the common defense, promote the general welfare, and secure the blessings of liberty to ourselves and our posterity,"[19] in one way or another.

> The *rationale* (rash - uh - nal ... with the accent on the last syllable, which rhymes with *pal*) is the fundamental reason for something; the logical basis.

When you enter the professional practice, appellate justices, trial judges, opposing counsel, co-counsel, and clients will continually expect you to ground your explanations and arguments in policy—to explain the underlying social utility for application of a particular law in lieu of an available alternative, for example. So also, as you practice law in law school, your professors will expect you to explain the policy-related rationale behind your analysis. Mere mechanistic application of sterile rules to culled facts gets the job done but is perceived as shallow. As you read appellate court opinions, particularly those of the United States Supreme Court, you will notice that most of them ground their decisions firmly on one or more socially appealing policies. Therefore, for each rule you have noted in your summary, search your notes for the fundamental policy rationale behind that rule, and include it.

Step Seven—Add cases as examples of how legal rules apply to specific factual scenarios

When writing examination answers, you need not include or refer to many of the cases found in your casebooks.

It may surprise you that the names of cases are the last bit of information in each [course summary] entry. That is because the individual cases are usually not very important. Some professors suggest that you can use the cases on an exam as a shorthand for a particular legal idea. Very few will expect you to know more than a very few important cases in detail in most of your substantive courses. The exceptions are Civil Procedure, Constitutional Law and Criminal Procedure, where Supreme Court cases dominate.[20]

Those few cases which merit specific references will be highlighted by your professors' frequent reference to them throughout the course or by the direct instruction, "you should remember this case." Of course, those cases deserve special emphasis in your course summary. Many of the other cases, however, serve as superb examples of rules and how they are applied. Although it is a fine idea to refer to such exemplar cases, avoid the temptation to import entire briefs—or major sections of briefs—into your course summary. Your immediate objective in briefing each case was considerably different than your reason for including the case in your summary; your case references should reflect that distinction.

Let *concision* and *precision* be your watchwords.

Step Eight—Format to manifest hierarchical alignment

By this point in the process you will have arranged the rules, exceptions, definitions, and related material into a sensible strata of classifications and categories (fundamental rules and their subordinates). Using your preferred method, arrange the text in your summary to visually reflect this hierarchical structure. Many students use classic techniques they learned in secondary or undergraduate school—Roman numerals for major headings, upper case letters for level two, Arabic numerals for level three, and so on, indenting each level a few spaces. Other students rely on different font choices (upper case, bold, italics, point-size differences), bullets and indentations to demonstrate the different levels. This is another place where you may choose to demonstrate categorization and subordination by the application of colors—colored fonts or highlighting for example. Design a visually effective method and stick with it throughout the summary.

Many law students use "Inspiration" software to create course summaries. This product is designed to provide a high-level outlining capability that automatically transforms the outline into a flow chart (or visa versa). See http://www.inspiration.com for details.

Step Nine—Revise as necessary

As you learn more, review concepts and cases, and experience the inevitable "aha!" moments and doctrinal epiphanies which erupt throughout every law student's first year, you will discover the need to rework parts of your summaries. These revisions should range from minor additions or word changes, to major overhauls of structure and substance. Do not be concerned if you return several times to "early" portions of each summary to revise—this is part of the process in which you are engaging, and it is a basic component of this self-instructional modality. This summary is your masterwork for you alone. You need to produce your finest work. Make your summary deep. Sharpen its analytical focus. Continually keep in mind that the summary is assessment-targeted, and should, therefore, represent direct doctrinal/analytical paths to high-level legal, cogent writing of examination answers.

Step Ten—Verify the summary's completeness and usefulness

If your summary is effective, it should help you navigate through your professor's examination questions. Road test its navigational capabilities. Try it out as you answer practice hypotheticals in writing each week (the seventh component of assessment-targeted study), and adjust it as necessary.

As you use your summary to assist you in responding in writing to practice hypothetical questions, you will notice that the summary will begin to communicate with you. It will *tell* you what you need to commit to memory, where you need to fill gaps (in your summary and in your comprehension), and most importantly, it will tell you where your analytical strengths and weaknesses lie. Listen to your course summary. Your course summary should "communicate" with you.

Here are examples of what will *not* qualify as a communicative course summary—precisely because they have no voice and remain passive and silent:

> Be aware that some professors allow students to use their course summaries when answering "take-home" final examinations; some allow course summaries to be used in the examination room. Check your course syllabi. Don't be misled, however. Your course summary may be a helpful tool during such an examination—but the *real* value comes from the active learning involved in the *production* of that tool.

- A copy of the table of contents from your casebook.
- A mere extraction of the points listed in the course syllabus.
- A list of cases studied and/or rules derived from those cases.
- Long summaries or explanations copied from commercial outlines, nutshells or hornbooks.

These you cannot "listen" to. You need to compose rich, deep, material that speaks to you and guides you as you write examination answers.

Before reading week arrives, your course summaries should be complete and, quite literally, dog-eared. Before reading week, each course summary should evolve into a flow-chart, a tool that spotlights and interweaves the issues that drive the course.

> A "dog-eared" book is one with corners of the leaves turned down, generally by readers. The turned down corners look somewhat like the floppy ears of a dog.

Component 5
Prepare Flow Charts

Practicing Lawyers Use Flow Charts

A new lawyer's first day at the Denver office of Banks, Strong & Padareski included a tour of the renovated space. Once a warehouse for a variety of industrial concerns, this three-story brick and board building was just the place for a firm which—for all its thirty years—had eschewed the "brass and glass" of the city office buildings.

As Barbara Martinez was led down the hardwood hallway, she caught a glimpse of a man with his blue shirt sleeves rolled up to the elbows, his red and black striped tie not quite cinched tight, drawing a cartoon on the wall with a fat green marking pen.

"Who is that fellow, and what's he doing in there?" Barbara asked her tour guide, a paralegal introduced only as "Skip."

"I'm sure he'd be happy to explain, Barbara." After tapping gently on the doorframe to catch his attention, Skip announced, "Mr. Padareski, this is Barbara Martinez, the new associate from Southern California. She's wondering why you're drawing that cartoon. I told her you'd explain."

After a few pleasantries, the exuberant trial lawyer told Barbara about his method of trial preparation—"Total mastery of every fact, every law, and every conflicting recollection of every witness," he boasted. "When I arrive at the courthouse, it's as if the case unfolding before the jury is an adaptation of a book I've written and a screenplay I've collaborated on."

After that introduction, Mr. Padareski ("call me Will") concisely explained his method.

The twenty-foot west wall of his office was made of drywall covered with burlap fabric. He pointed out the 3 by 5-inch cards he had fastened across the top of the wall with push-pins. "These are the elements of my case," he said as he gestured to cards reading "Duty," "Breach of Duty," "Causation," and "Damages."

As he gestured with his palm, Barbara's eyes followed three strands of red string leading from the "Breach" card to the three smaller cards on the wall. "And these," Will emphasized with a nearly balletic flourish, "are the three separate negligent acts of the company we're suing."

The trial attorney went on to show Barbara how each of the smaller cards was connected by strings to other sets of cards below, representing elemental facts and names of the witnesses who would establish those facts in the trial next month. The cartoons were Will's basic caricatures of the witnesses.

"It looks," Barbara observed, "like a schematic diagram, or an illustrated family tree."

"Precisely," Will explained, "and by constantly rearranging the 'limbs' and 'leaves' until I get the perfectly sculpted 'tree,' I become so familiar with every tiny element of my case—and its relation to every other element—that I present most of the trial without referring to notes. Especially," he smiled, "the closing argument, which I always deliver with the passion I can only muster when I know every tiny detail of the case by heart."

Barbara Martinez thanked Will Padareski for the explanation then continued on down the hall with Skip—never mentioning that she had been using a similar device all through law school. Her academic support mentor had called it the "Subject-Specific Wall Chart." That, she kept to herself, was the secret to her top ten percent ranking and would be the mainstay of her litigation career. It was foolproof.

Lawyers often use flow charts to work through difficult material, to assist them in their legal writing, and to present concepts to others. "On occasion," explains an article in the *Los Angeles Lawyer* magazine, "there is a need for illustrating logical information in a case or trans-action that can facilitate communication with client, colleague, opposing counsel, or the court." The author recommends construction of flow charts, "to show logical relations and logical steps which must be taken for a given set of circumstances," for example, to illustrate elements of a claim, the flow of a lawsuit (from the filing of a complaint through trial procedures), the facts of a case, the relationships of parties, and complex business interrelationships.[21]

Several trial attorneys writing in The Association of Trial Lawyers of America monthly magazine explained that, because "humans are visual animals ... [and] visual images penetrate the mind with immediacy that aural and verbal stimuli cannot match," they recommend flow charting as a visual strategy to help jurors organize the facts presented during a jury trial.[22] Similarly, a 2002 practice guide for California civil trial lawyers, written by lawyers and judges, cites the use of flow charts as helpful visual aids during opening statements at the commencement of civil jury trials.[23]

Lawyers use flow charts to assist them in constructing written arguments as well. Professor Laurie Zimet of Hastings College of Law, writing for the Practicing Law Institute, explains, "Thinking and plan-ning ... are the foundations of good writing.... A number of people like to use a long roll of paper for a flow chart approach...."[24] The intricate, sophisticated "if-then" thinking within the realm of categories and consequences often requires the use of some form of visual representation to comprehend, clarify, organize, and communicate ideas to lawyers, between lawyers, and from lawyers to others.

Start Practicing Now: Prepare Flow Charts

Successful law students discover that *organization* is the key to learning *and* to demonstrating to professors (in essay examination answers) that they are able to weave through the maze of legal rules, exceptions, definitions, and policies *deftly*, to provide cogent written resolutions to complex problems posed by the professors. Yes, organization is the key to learning.

- One must *remember* information in order to *use* it.
- One must *understand* information in order to *remember* it.
- One must structurally *organize* information to *understand* it—continually integrating new information with known information.

As legal principles are inductively derived from the court opinions studied for each class, they tend to tumble into student consciousness in an untidy, jumbled heap. Without structure, they remain that way. As soon as the information becomes comprehensible—not later—students need to immediately arrange it into meaningful structures. The process of learning law necessarily includes the process of building a complex latticework of corelevant, interdependent, hierarchical structures of principles, categories, and consequences.

Powerful learning occurs when new information is assimilated into existing cognitive structures.[25] If each chunk of new material is summarized, then extracted from the course summary and retooled to fit precisely into a pre-existing design, logical links are forged—links which will eventually provide the roadmap through an entire course and serve as the graphic design for matchless examination answers.

These legal roadmaps—which first serve as learning devices, then evolve quickly into exam answer templates—are flow charts.

Referring to the ability to draw graphic organizers as "an extraordinarily valuable learning tool for law students,"[26] Professor Wangerin explains that flow charts "provide students with a learning tool that allows the students to create visual images of the handful of core principles that link seemingly unrelated bits of knowledge. By forcing students to draw visual images of core ideas, therefore, graphic organizers help students develop constructed knowledge."[27]

> Dean Roach writes, "With regard to properly preparing for exams, many of my students report that flow charting is the single most useful learning strategy they learned in the academic support program." Cathaleen A. Roach, *A River Runs Through It*, 36 Ariz. L. Rev. 667, 691 (1994).

Nuts and Bolts: Preparing Flow Charts

Flow charts are course schematics, built piece by piece, week by week, topic by topic. Professionals and academics have been using flow charts for years to demonstrate processes, governmental structures, and information streams. Thus, many different types of charts have been developed, and are now rather standardized. They appear in college textbooks in nearly every discipline. Follow these four steps *weekly* to create your flow chart in each subject:

> You are probably quite familiar with the "spider map," the "series of events chain," the "fishbone map," the "cycle map," and the "network tree" although you may not recognize them by these esoteric names. If you are interested, a quick Internet web search will lead you to examples.

1. Extract the issue-resolving questions from your course summary.
2. Arrange the questions in a systematic, hierarchical schematic structure.
3. Use the flow chart to answer single-issue hypothetical questions.
4. Modify the flow chart as needed; extend it weekly.

Step One—Extract the issue-resolving questions from your course summary

Your course summary is the platform from which the flow chart is generated. This is the starting place—your powerful summary of the course as taught by your professor, as interpreted by you, completely in line with the authorities you have consulted and summarized. If you prepare your summary on a weekly basis, you should have a brief segment completed on a single topic or a few subtopics. For example, in Contracts class, you may have just dealt with the elements of an "offer" to engage in a contractual relationship. If those elements made up the readings and discussion for the week, those are the items you will have just detailed in your course summary, and those are the items you should then add to your flow chart.

Your course summary will probably include primarily declaratory sentences (simple, direct statements of fact). But lawyers are questioners. Lawyers ask questions of themselves, each other, and witnesses. Lawyers ask "rhetorical questions" to juries and judges. For example, in her closing argument to a jury, a criminal defense lawyer may say, "Ladies and gentlemen, I ask you, did the prosecutor prove beyond any reasonable doubt that my client murdered Mr. Oliphant?" ... then she will proceed to explain ... "You can only answer that question 'yes' if you first answer this question, 'Did the defendant *intend to kill* Mr. Oliphant?' Have you heard one peppercorn of evidence—one shred of testimony—one fragment of information that would lead you to believe that my client wanted to see Mr. Oliphant dead? No. Nada. Not any!"

What is this defense lawyer doing? She is doing precisely what she did in law school. She is following the template, the systematic, logical hierarchical order of the essential legal questions that must be answered

> One party to a contract, the "offeror" makes an "offer" to the other (referred to as the "offeree") when she manifests a willingness to enter into a bargain with the other person, sufficiently clear to justify that person's belief that his assent to the bargain will result in a contract. The terms of the offer must meet certain minimum objective standards, for example, reasonable specificity as to its basic terms—price, description, and time for performance. The essential components of an "offer" are its "elements." Thus, the question of whether any given series of words or statements or inquiries constitutes an "offer"—that is, includes the requisite elements—occupies considerable time in a first-year student's study of this area of law.

by applying the facts to resolve a puzzling inquiry. Questions. It's all about questions.

Construct your flow chart as a series of questions. Why? Asking and answering questions impels you to think like a lawyer. More importantly (for achieving your shorter-term goal of achieving your personal best grades on law school examinations), this method drives the exam answer writing process by forcing you to spot every issue the professor has imbedded in the exam question and by encouraging you to extract every available fact to use to your advantage in your analysis of how to resolve each issue.

How does declarative material in your course summary morph into essential questions? Consider the following example. In Torts class you will learn that a homeowner is responsible to keep his property in a safe condition, so visitors avoid injury. Once in a while, someone will visit, cut his hand on a broken faucet handle, receive a serious burn from an exposed wire, or get gnawed by a dangerous pet. Do these unfortunates have legal redress against the homeowner? In many states, that depends on their "status" during their visit. Those invited as guests, those entering for business purposes, and those entering without any permission (burglars for example) are subject to different rules. The homeowner owes a higher duty of care to someone she has invited to her home to discuss selling that home, than she does to someone who enters her home for the purpose of kidnapping her. The complicated rules, exceptions, explanations, rationales, public policies, and economic considerations for this area of the law should be detailed over several pages in a law student's course summary. But the bare-bones questions that need to be addressed will be pointed and specific.

- Is plaintiff a trespasser?
- Is plaintiff a licensee?
- Is plaintiff an invitee?

The first question ("Is plaintiff a trespasser?") cannot be answered without knowing certain elemental information. In order to determine if the plaintiff trespassed, certain specific questions need to be answered— and if the answers to these questions lead one to believe that plaintiff was indeed a trespasser, answers to additional questions will help clarify whether the plaintiff is entitled to some special consideration, taking her outside of the normal rules.

Examples of the questions lawyers, law professors and law students will ask in the area of the duty (responsibility) owed to a trespassing plaintiff include ...

- Did she enter the land with permission?
- Was the permission express?
- Was the permission implied?
- Did she enter under some kind of legal privilege?
- At the time, was she a public safety officer? ... A census taker? ... A reporter?
- Was she acting within the course and scope of her employment?
- Did she exceed the scope of her employment?
- Was she "discovered" by the homeowner?
- Was there any form of adequate warning posted?
- Was the plaintiff a child at the time of the entry?

> See the two partially completed flow charts at the end of this section for illustrations of steps one and two.

Answers to these questions (as applicable to the situation at hand) are essential to resolve the problem. But these questions seem *random*, don't they?

Step Two—Arrange the questions in a systematic, hierarchical schematic structure

Lawyerly analysis requires systematic inquiry. Therefore, your flow chart must be systematic—it must be a coherent and interdependent group of factual questions that methodically lead to the resolution of a legal inquiry.

> The word "systematic" is derived from Greek words meaning "to stand" and "to combine"—the combination of questions you are building when you construct the systematic flow chart provides the legs upon which your legal argument (which you will make in your examination answer, then later, in court) will stand.

The system involved is one of categories and consequences: if this, then that. In court, the efficient lawyer will often lead a witness along a systematic path: if—then—then what—then what? The lawyer never gets to the second question if the first question isn't answered with the information that logically leads to the second question. Perhaps you can recall from films or television courtroom dramas, when one attorney objects, "Your Honor, that question is irrelevant!" The judge often turns to the lawyer who asked the question and inquires, "Counsel, where is all this leading? How is this relevant?" What the judge is really saying is, "We don't see how the answer to this last question you have asked will supply information which will help to resolve the legal question we are now trying to resolve." To overcome the objection, the lawyer needs to (metaphorically speaking) draw a flow chart for the judge, to demonstrate how the answer to the proffered question may provide a necessary link or bridge to the next logical step in the argument she intends to build.

Lawyerly analysis also requires that the "system" of inquiries be *hierarchical* in nature. This means that the questions need to be arranged in a ranked order, with subordinate questions preceded by the major questions. For example, when dealing with the question of the liability of an alleged homeowner to one who sustains an injury inside the alleged homeowner's house, the first question to answer is whether the defendant is indeed the owner of the house. Only after that has been established does the remaining series of questions make sense. If, for example, the defendant was merely a casual *visitor* to the house, all further questions along this line of inquiry are irrelevant, since the defendant could not possibly be liable under a homeowner liability theory. Of course, if the answer to the question is "no," the defendant may still be liable for plaintiff's injury—but that liability would fall under an entirely different system of questions. If the answer to the question is "yes," then the next question to be asked may be, "What was the 'status' of the plaintiff?" Why is that the *next* question? Because, in order to determine what level of responsibility the homeowner had to the plaintiff, in a state that allows for different levels of responsibility (or "duty"), the court needs to know what the plaintiff was doing inside the home. If he was a burglar, the homeowner may owe him no duty whatsoever; if he was there to repair the plumbing, the homeowner may owe him a much higher level of responsibility (for example, to warn him of the dangerous bare electrical wires in the basement). If he was there to repair the plumbing, the next series of questions may relate to whether, at the time of the injury, he was repairing the plumbing or engaged in some activity outside the scope of his plumbing repair mission. If, for example, his plumbing task was to take place upstairs in the laundry room, and he had migrated to the basement—without authorization—to browse through the homeowner's collection of stuffed parrots, perhaps his "status" had temporarily changed.

> Certainly, the homeowner's lawyer will be arguing to the court that, although the homeowner may have had a high degree of responsibility to keep the *work area* relatively safe for the plumber, there was no obligation to warn him of dangerous conditions in a part of the house the plumber was not authorized to visit.

One question *follows* another. Basic legal analysis follows a predictable path. When you construct your flow chart in a systematic and hierarchical pattern, you are laying the stepping stones along that path. It is upon these stones that you will eventually walk, as you walk your professor through your analytically efficient legal argument presented in your examination answer.

Step Three—Use the flow chart to answer single-issue hypothetical questions

> Where do you find these questions? Turn to the section on the seventh Law CAT, "Practice Answering Hypotheticals in Writing."

Having constructed a segment of your flow chart, test its functionality and efficiency by using it to answer single-issue hypothetical questions. With your flow chart in front of you, walk through the answers to several exam-type hypothetical questions that specifically deal with the area you have just charted. The chart should guide you through a highly efficient analysis of the facts presented in the hypothetical and lead you to a defensible conclusion. At *this* point, however, you need not answer hypotheticals in writing since you are only testing the efficacy of the flow chart (rather than putting your *self* to the test). Oral (audible) or mental (silent) answers will suffice—you will know right away if you need to adjust your chart by adding more questions or by changing the hierarchical structure.

Step Four—Modify the flow chart as needed; extend it weekly

The flow charts you create for individual issues, for discrete segments of each course, should be integrated into your schematic for the entire course as the course evolves and unfolds from week to week. For example, in Contracts class you may discover that the major elements required in a contract include an offer, an acceptance, and consideration. Although you may spend several weeks in class dealing with different modes of "acceptance" and thus develop a sophisticated flow chart devoted to that topical area, you will need to integrate that into the "larger picture" so that you are acutely aware of the position of "acceptance" in the grand scheme of contract law. That is, no one really cares much about whether there was an acceptance until it is established that there was an "offer." Without an "offer," a person has nothing to "accept." This, then, is an example of the "hierarchy" concept—the "offer" set of questions needs to be asked and answered *before* the "acceptance" set of questions becomes relevant. By integrating each distinct segment into the full schematic, you will never lose sight of where you *are* in the course—or in your analysis.

Further, as you add to your flow chart, and continue to test its usefulness, you will continue to patch holes in it. As your legal acumen becomes more sophisticated, you will undoubtedly notice the need for adjustment and fortification of your flow charts.

Each week, as you attend to this process of integration, adjustment and fortification, you will be extending your flow chart, so that it eventually covers every segment of the course as taught by your professor and as augmented by your own input.

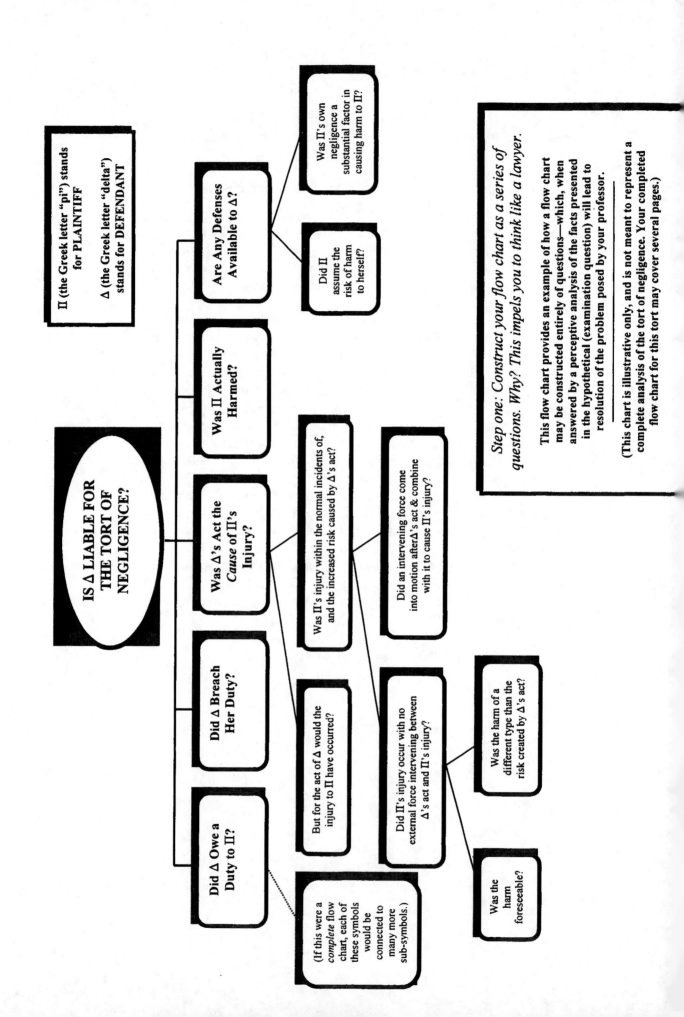

Π (the Greek letter "pi") stands for PLAINTIFF

Δ (the Greek letter "delta") stands for DEFENDANT

IS Δ LIABLE FOR THE TORT OF NEGLIGENCE?

Did Δ Owe a Duty to Π?

Did Δ Breach Her Duty?

Was Δ's Act the *Cause* of Π's Injury?

Was Π Actually Harmed?

Are Any Defenses Available to Δ?

Did Π assume the risk of harm to herself?

Was Π's own negligence a substantial factor in causing harm to Π?

But for the act of Δ would the injury to Π have occurred?

Was Π's injury within the normal incidents of, and the increased risk caused by Δ's act?

Did an intervening force come into motion after Δ's act & combine with it to cause Π's injury?

Did Π's injury occur with no external force intervening between Δ's act and Π's injury?

Was the harm of a different type than the risk created by Δ's act?

Was the harm foreseeable?

(If this were a *complete* flow chart, each of these symbols would be connected to many more sub-symbols.)

Step one: Construct your flow chart as a series of questions. Why? This impels you to think like a lawyer.

This flow chart provides an example of how a flow chart may be constructed entirely of questions—which, when answered by a perceptive analysis of the facts presented in the hypothetical (examination question) will lead to resolution of the problem posed by your professor.

(This chart is illustrative only, and is not meant to represent a complete analysis of the tort of negligence. Your completed flow chart for this tort may cover several pages.)

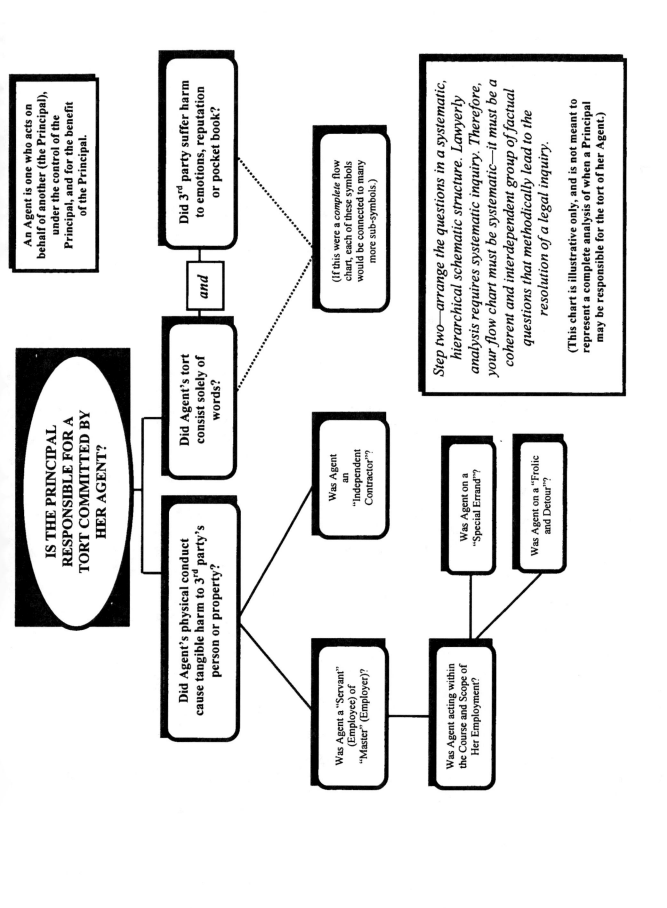

An Agent is one who acts on behalf of another (the Principal), under the control of the Principal, and for the benefit of the Principal.

IS THE PRINCIPAL RESPONSIBLE FOR A TORT COMMITTED BY HER AGENT?

Did Agent's tort consist solely of words?

Did 3rd party suffer harm to emotions, reputation or pocket book?

and

(If this were a *complete* flow chart, each of these symbols would be connected to many more sub-symbols.)

Did Agent's physical conduct cause tangible harm to 3rd party's person or property?

Was Agent an "Independent Contractor"?

Was Agent a "Servant" (Employee) of "Master" (Employer)?

Was Agent acting within the Course and Scope of Her Employment?

Was Agent on a "Special Errand"?

Was Agent on a "Frolic and Detour"?

Step two—arrange the questions in a systematic, hierarchical schematic structure. Lawyerly analysis requires systematic inquiry. Therefore, your flow chart must be systematic—it must be a coherent and interdependent group of factual questions that methodically lead to the resolution of a legal inquiry.

(This chart is illustrative only, and is not meant to represent a complete analysis of when a Principal may be responsible for the tort of her Agent.)

Component 6
Internalize

Practicing Lawyers Internalize Data

Law students visiting the ceremonial State Supreme Court courtroom marveled (as did opposing counsel) at Patrick Wu's near legendary ability to speak at length without notes. Not only could he state convoluted propositions of law in exquisitely simple and dignified language, but he also demonstrated an uncanny capability to recall case names, holdings, and words from statutes when responding to the questions he was peppered with by the honorable justices.

Shortly before Rosalie Raponi's first appellate argument, she walked down the hallway to Patrick's office to ask him to divulge his secret.

"Oh, it's not any special gift, Rosalie," the senior partner explained, "it's just a matter of becoming wholly familiar with every minute aspect of the case—of every pertinent trial exhibit, every case cited by either party in the written briefs, and all the twists and turns."

"But how," the younger associate inquired, "do you memorize all that?"

"I don't 'memorize' it in the way that you're thinking of it, Rosalie," he continued, "I internalize it. There's a difference." Patrick went on to explain what he meant. "By the time I filed the Appellant's Opening Brief with the Supreme Court, it included 40 cases in support of my position. Those 40 represent only the most persuasive—I'd read and summarized hundreds of cases, including all those I expect the Respondent to use."

Moving out from behind his desk, Patrick began to pace around the office as he went on. "By the time I filed that first brief in this case, Rosalie, I had read, scrutinized, analyzed, digested, summarized, and virtually autopsied every court opinion which might be important to my case. The most important decisions, I know almost as well as if I'd written them myself. You see, Rosalie, for me, each case now 'lives' within a context. The legal theories, the testimony of witnesses, the facts of the case, and the documents admitted as evidence—for me, they're woven neatly together to form the fabric of my case." He paused to let this sink in, then revealed another strategy.

"However, I must admit" he said, with a slight smile, "I've always had a bit of difficulty with case name, and with numbers—like what year an opinion was written or some of the numbers involved in the case itself. So those, I just out-and-out memorize."

"And how do you go about that," Rosalie pressed.

"Well, don't tell anyone, but I use the same methods I used in high school history class—flashcards. For those names and numbers which just refuse to settle in to my long-term memory, I write them down on little cards, which I review every once in a while. Believe me, no one ever sees me with those little cards, and they hit the trash can immediately after I deliver my argument."

Rosalie was startled to discover that the senior appellate advocate at Wu, Nolan & Genova used the same method that she had used as a first-year law student, and she silently thanked him for reminding her of just how effective it had been. She remembered that most of the essentials of Torts and Contracts had become part of her daily language, as she gained fluency in the language of the law through continual input and output throughout the semester. But for the terms, definitions, exceptions to rules, and a few case names, she had created a set of personal flash cards—they had worked wonders to dispel all vestiges of exam anxiety and had helped her achieve her place in the top quartile of her class.

Patrick Wu had just given her the boost she needed to use the same methods to relieve much of the anxiety she was feeling as she headed for her first appellate oral argument.

Simply put, a "mnemonic" is a memory tool. Many practicing lawyers use mnemonic devices to assure them of instant recall of essential matters when they are under pressure. In *The Lore and Literature of Advocacy*, lawyers Michael and Jane Tigar explain to appellate attorneys, that "one might use mnemonic devices," for example, creating verbal "markers" that can be easily recalled during oral argument, including "vivid words, or particular forms of expressions."[28]

Trial lawyers use memory tools to remember key elements of closing arguments and even to prepare snap responses for often-used courtroom objections.

Most lawyers are quite familiar with mnemonics and the important role they play when instant recall under stress is essential: bar examination preparation courses are replete with memory devices.[29]

Mnemonic devices are often "short term" memory aids. The longer-term recollection comes from true "internalization," that is, by incorporating information into one's personal store of knowledge—an integral element of achieving fluency in the language of the law.

"BARPH," explains a U.S. Army litigator, "is a mnemonic device to assist trial advocates in remembering the different foundations that are commonly required for documentary evidence: Best evidence, Authentication, Relevance, Privilege, and Hearsay.... The mnemonic enhances trial advocacy by arming counsel with the ability to respond quickly with the possible objections to documents." Major Grammel, *The Art of Trial of Advocacy: Worried About Objecting to a Document? Just BARPH*, ARMY LAW, Feb. 2000, at 28.

Start Practicing Now: Internalize

Professor John Delaney, in his classic *How to do Your Best on Law School Exams*, explains the importance of memorization:

Always keep in mind that mnemonics ... and related techniques encode data, not knowledge, and certainly not understanding. Stated differently, memory techniques encode doctrine as data, but your objective always is to encode doctrine as knowledge and understanding. Since you are unlikely to extract from your short-and-long-term memory more than what you have encoded, you will be careful not to reduce your learning to encoding data alone. In my experience, this reduction disables the learning of some law students. But positively, encoding data in mnemonics and related techniques can work well if such techniques are a part of a larger encoded knowledge and understanding.[30]

Professor Stephen Emanuel, in *Getting Great Grades with Law in a Flash* (an instruction book for his company's flash card series), insists that "There are certain things you have to memorize ... (1) A general topic outline of your course; (2) Every major element and standard; (3) how to apply those elements and standards to facts."[31] He points out that "memorizing rules ... remove[s] the possibility that you will have to waste time on remembering rules during the exam."[32]

Dr. Mary Campbell Gallagher,[33] an expert at bar examination preparation, is blunt about the importance of memorizing when it comes to preparing for bar examinations: "[I]n order to state the law, you must know the law. And the way to know the rules of law is to memorize them. To score high on the essay part of the bar examination, you must memorize the basic rules of law ...."[34]

Despite the apparent conspicuity of the proposition that one must commit to memory what one needs to write with automaticity and rapidity during a stressful, timed, brief, writing session—nevertheless, law professors around the country bristle when they hear students being counseled to "memorize." This opposition to memorizing, perhaps related to the professorial tendency to view law study as a deductive exercise, is pervasive and (according to Dr. Gallagher) imposed unfairly upon law students, for whom "it pays to memorize." Dr. Gallagher counsels, "Memorization is your friend. It pays in law school and it pays off on the bar examination—handsomely."[35]

Do not be swayed by educational philosophy or pedagogic prejudices advanced by professors who think that "memorize" is a dirty word. These same professors expect their students to accurately state difficult rules of law, remember the elements of many crimes and torts, and respond automatically to certain verbal triggers.

Professor Wangerin points out that "verbatim knowledge ... is, in fact, extremely important in virtually all law school classes because verbatim knowledge serves as the foundation for all other learning."[36]

Be careful not to confuse the need for instant, automatic recall of words, phrases, and definitions with "parroting" of the law. "Your job," Professor Corinne Cooper explains, "is finding a balance. Learn the meaning of each new word or term and use it with precision, but do not memorize endless phrases and parrot them back." Corinne Cooper, *Letter to a Young Law Student*, 35 Tulsa L.J. 275, 285–86 (2000). The words you will eventually write in your exam bluebook will *include* the words you have learned by heart, but they will constitute only a portion of the analytical presentation you will develop.

Professor Kissam counsels students that "internalization of doctrine requires at least some memorization of rules."[37] Commitment of the rules, definitions, exceptions, and other essential material to memory, so that these words, phrases, maxims and even templates for persuasive arguments become an integral part of your legal vocabulary, is essential in order to achieve the liberating degree of instant automaticity you will need. Need? Yes, in order to spend your precious limited exam answering time on the essential activities of analysis and persuasive writing, you *need* to be in a position to spend no appreciable time groping for essentials.

Nuts and Bolts: Internalizing

The internalization objective includes two major aspects: the development of instant automaticity and the construction of an infallible issue index.

Development of instant automaticity

In law school, "automaticity" refers to the spontaneous utterance (or writing) of predetermined rules, rubrics, definitions, legal expressions, and terms of art. Here are some examples:

- You will discover that some contracts must be "evidenced by a writing signed by the parties sought to be bound."
- You will learn that, in order for a civil court to have the power to render a judgment affecting a defendant, in some circumstances, the court must find that "the defendant purposely availed himself of the privilege of conducting activities within the forum state, thus invoking the benefits and protections of its laws."
- You will encounter the tort of assault and be expected to remember that one element of this intentional tort is "an act by the defendant creating a reasonable apprehension in plaintiff of immediate harmful or offensive contact to plaintiff's person."

For each class you need to master the vocabulary—words, phrases, clauses and sentences—associated with each area of the law. Remember, the objective of assessment-targeted study is to be able to demonstrate fluency in the language of the law when it counts—on the final examination. Fluency in any language implies the ability to produce key words and phrases without searching the mind—*automatically*.

Construction of an infallible issue index

Answering law school essay examinations includes recognition of legal "issues"—vexing problems that lawyers see as resolvable by application of legal rules. Often, these issues lurk hidden within a complex fictional narrative presented as a problem that needs to be resolved. *Before* the issues can be addressed by application of the appropriate rules, they need to be ferreted out from the narrative. During the stress of exams, agitated students, in an urgent race against the clock, often overlook even obvious issues. This common misfortune can be entirely avoided by the simple internalization of an issue checklist. Most every professor will test only on issues she suspects will be recognizable to her students—those covered in the classroom or by required reading. A simple checklist of issues, against which any exam question can be compared, provides the antidote to issue evaporation.

Three steps to developing instant automaticity

Fluency presupposes mastery of the lexicon of the standard expressions, as well as the syntax of how those expressions are best woven together, to produce the fabric of a persuasive legal analysis. Therefore, you must practice. Practicing produces lexical and syntactical proficiency. Just as mastery of a foreign language requires continual practice (immersion), mastery of writing fluently in the language of the law results from continual practice. In addition to creating course summaries and flow charts:

- Write responses to all practice exams your professors provide for you.
- Write answers to short, single-issue, hypothetical questions found in commercial sources.
- Exchange questions with fellow students; then exchange answers.
- Engage in all exam-writing workshops and simulated examination opportunities offered by your school's Academic Support Program.

While some students seem to pick up the jargon almost intuitively, as some students pick up French or Japanese almost intuitively, most need to expend significant effort to acquire the language of the law, and to write it with the ease, aplomb, and authority. Undertake the process of acquiring instant automaticity methodically, in stages. Consider these steps:

Step One—Determine which words and expressions you need to automatize, each week

As a general rule, what you need to automatize should be very evident from your readings and from class (mostly from class). Most law professors repeat, emphasize, and sometimes write on the board those expressions they expect students to know "by heart." At some point in class, you will hear your Contracts professor say something to this effect: "To decide whether an 'offer' creates a reasonable expectation in the offeree that the offeror is willing to enter into a contract, courts will generally ask three questions: (1) Was there an expression of a *promise, undertaking, or commitment* to enter into a contract? (2) Were there *certainty and definiteness* in the essential terms? (3) Was there *communication* of the foregoing to the offeree?" You will probably also notice that these questions appear on a handout, in your book, or on the blackboard. Similarly, in a Property class, while studying the doctrine of "adverse possession," you may learn that such possession must be "continuous, hostile, open, actual, notorious and exclusive." These words and phrases that are immediately recognizable as elemental and essential law are words and phrases that you must include in your basic legal lexicon and use properly as you write and speak. Mark these expressions as they appear in your course summary. That way, each week, you will augment your essential legal lexicon with the expressions that were used by your professor and which you recognized as important.

Step Two (optional)—select a mnemonic method

Mnemonic devices abound. Use of an Internet search engine will net significant results. Common mnemonic methods employed by law students are acronyms and acrostics.

Acronyms are formed from the first letters of each word in a group of words you need to remember. You are familiar with many acronyms already. For example, RAM is random access memory; SCUBA is self-contained underwater breathing apparatus. You can use *parts* of the words as well, not just the first letters. For example, RADAR is radio detecting and ranging. The resulting "word" can be a nonsense word, but it is one that is easy to remember. Law students sometimes use acronyms to remember strings of words or phrases representing elements of different legal theories or rules of law. For example, an acronym for the elements of adverse possession (above) could be "CHOANE," where each letter of the nonsense word corresponds to the first letter of a word you need to recall instantly. In your Torts class you may learn that a particular type of slander known as "slander *per se*" involves one of these topics: a criminal act, business reputation, impurity, or a disease

> *Mnemonic* (the "m" is silent) means "assisting the memory." The word is derived from the name of the Greek goddess of memory, Mnemosyne. Type combinations of these search words into your Internet search engine to find memory devices:
>
> - Mnemonic
> - Memorize
> - Memory techniques
> - Acronyms

exposed. One commercial study aid suggests you remember these with the acronym "CAB RIDE."[38]

Acrostics are formed by using the first letters of the words you need to remember, but using those letters to make a phrase or sentence instead of a word. You are probably familiar with many acrostics from earlier educational experiences. "Please excuse my dear Aunt Sally" is an acrostic many mathematics teachers employ to remind students of the order of operations in mathematics: parenthesis, exponents, multiplication and division from left to right, and addition and subtraction from left to right. In biology class, "King Phil Can Only find Green Snakes" reminds students of Kingdom, Phylum, Class, Order, Genus, Species. Perhaps you will remember the elements of common law burglary (Breaking and Entering the Dwelling of Another at Nighttime with the intent to commit a Felony therein) by remembering "Become Each Day A Never-Failer" or "Burglars Execute Daily A New Felony."

> Avoid overuse of mnemonic devices. The most solid and reliable memory power is produced by usage.

Mnemonic devices can clutter your mind. Consider using them only when essential—when you simply can*not* seem to remember the major exceptions to the hearsay rule, for example.

Step Three—Create personal flashcards rather than buying a commercially produced set

Flashcards are very powerful memory tools for some students. Cut unlined, blank 3 by 5-inch cards in half (producing 3 by 2½-inch cards) and write a single term on the front, with only the key words of the definition or the key elements of the tort (for example) on the back side. If you create a stack of cards for each subject, use the stack daily to reinforce your memory, *as you begin to study that subject*. If you create your personal set of flashcards weekly, using your freshly developed course summary as the source, you will *never* grope for words, phrases, definitions or elements. As your comfort level grows (that is, as you come to know the definitions and elements "by heart"), place the fully learned cards in one stack, and the yet-to-be-perfected cards in another. Watch the perfected stack grow. As you continually employ those words in your weekly speech and writing, the cards themselves will become superfluous artifacts long before exam day.

The ease of developing instant automaticity in the language of the law varies from student to student—just as with foreign language learning; some have an aptitude that facilitates faster development. As with most laudable pursuits, attainment depends in large measure on your passion, your persistence, the clarity of your vision, and your commitment to excellence.

The single step for construction of an infallible issue index is this: repeated use of your flow chart—every week in every subject. Initially, use it while looking at it, to resolve hypothetical problems. Rather quickly, wean yourself from the physical flow chart, and visualize it in your mind as you move from step to step of your analytical answer construction. The flow charts themselves will become your infallible checklist of all major and minor issues in every course.

Component 7
Practice Answering Hypotheticals
in Writing (Rehearse)

Practicing Lawyers Rehearse

"Ladies and gentlemen," the lanky second year associate intoned, "this week my task will be to convince you of the truth of the facts alleged in Mr. Fowler's complaint and to demonstrate how proper application of the law of this state to those facts will result in a verdict favoring my client, Mr. Fowler." A pleasant look, not quite a smile, but with a hint of self-assurance, graced his face as Peter Lasko continued with his opening statement.

Passing by the glass wall of the conference room, Diane Zabreski, the firm's newest addition as a paralegal, was baffled—"Why is that fellow speaking so solemnly to a potted palm?" she asked aloud.

Carlos, the lawyer taking Diane on her guided tour responded quickly, "That's how Peter prepares for trial—he rehearses all the important parts. Yesterday, he delivered the same opening statement to the receptionist and me; today, it's the potted palm. If the palm seems to like his revisions, I expect he'll pull me in to listen again this afternoon."

Later, Diane met Peter in the lunchroom. "Will you tell me about your rehearsals?" she inquired.

"Sure," Peter offered. "I suppose it's something I learned in high school drama. The drama teacher never let us put on a play without rehearsing. When I did public speaking in college, I always delivered my speech several times to whomever I could get to listen. In law school, by the time I appeared before the Appellate Advocacy Panel, I had delivered the Appellant's opening argument a dozen times. When I took my first real Torts exam—well, it wasn't my first ... it was about my fiftieth. Get the picture? Benjamin Franklin was right—practice makes perfect."

The next day, Diane was in the Whitman County Superior Court witnessing the same calm and confident young lawyer, Peter Lasko, deliver a superlative, relaxed, and very impressive opening statement to the jury. She was the only other one in the courtroom who knew that the potted palm had okayed the revisions—this opening was a rhetorical masterpiece.

Trial lawyers often rehearse opening statements, closing arguments, and particular questions (or lines of questioning) they intend to ask witnesses. Appellate lawyers practice their oral arguments prior to their actual appearances before the appellate justices. Witnesses who testify in court, particularly expert witnesses, have often rehearsed their testimony many times with the attorneys who call them to the stand. Many lawyers will videotape a key witness and play the tape back for the witness, providing essential feedback for the question, "How am I doing?" Some lawyers actually deliver their orations to an unoccupied courtroom, just before the actual event, simulating the actual experience as much as possible. It works out the kinks, gets rid of the butterflies, builds confidence, and makes for a smoother overall presentation, increasing the chances of achieving better results for the client. Rehearsal—practice— that's an integral part of the practice of law.

Start Practicing Now: Rehearse Your Examination Experience by Answering Practice Hypotheticals

Although an increasing number of law professors are including a variety of assessment tools in their first-year courses, the predominant first-year test is the so-called "blue book" exam, also referred to as the "essay" exam. The "blue book" exam is an "end-of-the-semester examination that counts for most or all of a student's grade and lasts no longer than a standard working day."[39] These exams typically require students to perform several intellectual functions and demonstrate that performance in clear, cogent writing.

A typical torts essay question, for example, will consist of several paragraphs of narrative about numerous parties who have inflicted and received a variety of injuries, followed by "the call of the question," in which the professor will call upon the law student to "analyze and discuss the respective rights and liabilities of each of the parties."

The first exam function is to "spot the issues," that is, determine which of the facts detailed in the long narrative raise "legal issues" or questions with which lawyers and courts will be concerned when attempting to resolve the controversies arising from the facts presented in the narrative. Each "issue" will usually consist of a question—for example, "Whether Maude's conduct was 'outrageous' under common law concepts, or merely impolite." The second examination function is to specify the particular legal rules, definitions, statutes, or holdings of precedential cases which apply to the issue and which will aid in its resolution. The third function requires the application of these rules and holdings to the facts, by integrating, or interweaving, the relevant facts with the elements of the rule.

Most examination questions will require (either expressly or impliedly) that the student present "both sides," that is, provide synthesized rule/fact analyses for each issue which may lead to opposing conclusions, then select the most likely conclusion, given generally recognized principles, precedents, or policies. The student is expected to employ these functional capabilities in writing which is persuasive and well-organized. Law professors expect exam answers to manifest a student's control of the material and to demonstrate her proficiency at succinct lawyerly writing.

Does this sound daunting? It should, because it is. However, as with most challenges you have encountered, the more you practice the specific tasks required, the less daunting the ultimate challenge becomes.

Within the context of law school, your target is a grade on your final examination that reflects your personal best: not your personal *unrehearsed* best, not your personal best under surprise conditions, but, rather, your personal best after an entire semester of preparation. Your professors *expect* you to practice writing examination answers. They are looking for fluency in the language of the law—specifically, in the language of the law of Torts, Contracts, or Civil Procedure. They expect you to write as if you are in total control of the language—and total control of *any* language is manifested by communication, in this case, communication of precise legal concepts and communication of a logical analysis supportive of a rational conclusion. The two (fluency and communication of concepts and analyses) are inextricably interwoven in the fabric of superb legal writing, as practiced by lawyers and judges. They should be interwoven in the fabric of your answer to each exam question.

Heed Professor Delaney's cautionary advice against a standard first-year student mistake: "Don't talk out your answers. Talking is worthwhile but can be misleading: you can inadvertently convince yourself that you know a segment of problems, issues and rules because you can talk about them, though you cannot identify issues, apply rules, interweave, etc., in lawyerly written form." Delaney, 54–55.

No one expects you to produce such a high end product without considerable practice. Nor should *you* have such expectations. Practice writing examination answers. Professor Delaney suggests, "You should practice these skills by writing succinct lawyerly answers with time pressure to problems from old exams, from your casebook ..." and from other sources.

Of all the Components of Assessment Targeted Study, rehearsing the examination experience is the most critical—and the most valuable. Rehearsal is the ultimate preparation. Realistically, there are only so many legal issues your professor can include in her examination, and the issues tested will be selected from the issues covered in class. If you have responded over and over to questions requiring you to analyze factual hypotheticals raising each of these issues, you will be prepared to do so again. You will have worked out all the "kinks" and be able to produce quality answers under examination conditions.

The rehearsal component of your study regimen can begin as soon as you have gathered enough material to begin analysis of hypothetical factual situations. For most first-year fall semester classes, this should occur after about three or four weeks. Although you won't be able to respond to full-blown final exam questions (since they will include problems too sophisticated for a novice to resolve), you will be able to adequately respond to questions aimed specifically at topics you have covered during the initial weeks of the course.

The questions you address should become increasingly more complex and should cover every issue studied in your course. By progressively increasing the difficulty level and coverage breadth of your practice questions, you will methodically strengthen your exam-taking capabilities. By the time you reach "reading week," you should be peaking—having answered dozens of questions over a period of more than two months, you will be fully prepared to answer just a few more, during the actual final examination.

Your exam-answering proficiency will evolve as you progress along the continuum leading to total fluency in the language of the law, and you will:

- Learn, employ and perfect exam-answering strategies.
- Imbed all important rules, exceptions, definitions, and policy statements in your long-term memory, for instant recall.
- Replace examination anxiety with excitement and eagerness.
- Assure yourself of performing at your highest levels on examination days.

Nuts and Bolts: Answering Practice Hypotheticals

You need to know where to find practice hypothetical questions, what to do with them once you have found them, and how to obtain feedback once you have answered them. Here are the nuts and bolts covering those three areas.

Where to find hypotheticals

First, a caveat: Not all hypothetical questions will be helpful. Even one of the best sources, your professor's old exam cache, may include questions raising issues your professor has decided not to cover in this particular semester. You must be careful to select questions keyed to your course coverage—if you encounter questions which require more legal knowledge than your professor expects you to have acquired, do not be discouraged—be realistic (move on). If you compare your course syllabus to a fully loaded commercial study aid for a first-year course, you will readily discern that your course covers only a percentage of issues, sub-issues, defenses, and policy considerations detailed in the commercial product. The four best sources to obtain practice hypothetical questions are your law school, commercial publications, your peers, and yourself.

Finding practice hypotheticals at your law school

In some classes, the best source of practice hypotheticals toward the *end* of the semester will be your professor. Every professor has a different philosophy of education and evaluation—many are quite helpful when it comes to providing students with exam insights, while others completely avoid that area of legal pedagogy. Professors who dispense practice examination questions usually do so in one or more of several different ways:

- *Class handouts.* Some professors will distribute practice exams at different stages throughout the course, or once near the middle of the semester, and encourage students to answer the questions under examination conditions. Often, one or more of those questions will be addressed by the professor in a subsequent class (or an after-class session), with an explanation of how a good answer should be developed.
- *Midterm examinations.* Find out if your professor intends to give a midterm examination to the class (also, find out if the exam will be graded and whether it will have any impact on your final grade). Whether it is to be a take-home exam, an in-class exam, graded or ungraded, plan on taking this examination. Often this is your professor's best attempt to offer you a preview of the type of examination she intends to present you with at the end of the semester.
- *Office handouts.* Plan on visiting the office of each of your professors during the semester. One of the questions you should ask is whether that professor will provide you with course-specific hypothetical questions for you to answer, and whether the professor will meet with you later, to go over the answers that you have written. Again, this is a question that will elicit a variety of answers from different professors.
- *In-class hypotheticals.* With little or no adjustment, the hypotheticals that your professor tosses out during every class provide near perfect single-issue practice examination questions. Your class notes should contain numerous hypotheticals from each class, many of which remain unanswered or only partially answered at the end of the class period. Rewrite the hypotheticals into succinct narratives, add a "call" inquiry or directive, and you will find that you have a superb custom-tailored issue-specific practice exam hypothetical question, illustrative of the way your professor designs examination questions.

> One professor may feel that providing supplemental material to a student during an office visit may amount to tilting the playing field in favor of students who visit the office; another professor may believe that those who seek additional assistance merit that assistance and will happily provide it.

A second source for potential practice examination questions at your law school is in your school's law library. It is common practice for law school libraries to keep indexed files filled with examinations each professor has given over the past several years. When you avail yourself of this source material, however, remember the caveats: these exams are probably too dense with legal problems for you to attack until the end of the course (trying to answer them sooner—besides being frustrating and demoralizing—will be unproductive in terms of achievement of your objective); also, the exam may cover material that your professor has not included in this semester's version of the course.

> *We believe that reviewing exams your professor has given in previous years (if they are available) is one of the most important things you can do to get ready for your finals.... Exams tend to cover issues the professor finds important or interesting, and these issues tend to remain similar from year to year. Neither the most thorough studying, the best commercial outline, nor even the best book on taking exams ... can substitute for insight into your professor's own approach ... looking at old exams can instill panic if done too early in the semester, when the questions are likely to seem unimaginably difficult. The answer here is to pick the right time somewhere near the end of the course but not too close to the end of your exam review.*[40]

Many schools have augmented or replaced their library exam bank files with computer accessible repositories. The same caveats apply.

Depending upon the level of Academic Support offered by your institution, you may discover that the Academic Support Program is a rich source of practice examinations. If the program is open to you, do not hesitate to visit and ask.

Finding practice hypotheticals in commercial publications

Most of your required texts ("casebooks") include factual scenarios after each topical subsection. The authors, editors, and publishers of these casebooks have expended quite a bit of effort to provide you with challenging problems, so you can exercise your skills and view the highlighted issue from several divergent perspectives. Although many students bypass these "problems" during their class preparation, they provide a rich resource for practicing law and for achieving fluency in the precise area of law that your professor wants you to focus on.

Quite a few commercial study aids supply an abundance of exam-like hypothetical questions. One of the beauties of the commercially produced questions is that they are often very, very issue-specific because that is how the books are set up. Examples of commercial publications that serve up a substantial supply of issue-specific, single or multiple-issue hypothetical questions—just what students need during the first ten weeks of the semester, include:

Check out the description of several commercial sources of hypotheticals in the supplement to this book.

- Steve Emanuel's *First Year Questions and Answers*. The questions are single and double-issue short essay types, not unlike some of the short questions many professors write for exams. This book also provides answers, with key words, phrases and terms of art in boldface and italics. The main text is preceded by a finely parsed and very reliable table of contents, which directs students to the precise questions that address the issues, sub-issues and subtleties encountered in their casebooks and classrooms. The answers, which you should read only after you have written out your own complete answers, are not only concise, but they are presented in a logical way that is not too different from the way students should present answers in examination situations. Keep in mind that these "answers" are not meant to be "model" answers for examination purposes, but, rather, explanations of the rules as they apply to the factual scenarios. The best "exam answer" may differ markedly from what Emanuel presents; however, Emanuel's basic analysis is generally quite reliable.
- *Examples and Explanations*. The Examples and Explanations series, published by Aspen Law & Business, includes most first-year subjects, and includes excellent, provocative topic-specific questions. The "explanations" offered in this series do not purport to be "model answers" but, rather, almost conversational explanations of how the law can resolve the sample problems.

Although the questions and answers proffered by the major players in the commercial study aid industry are (a) high-level and (b) continually scrutinized by legions of demanding law students, this is not the case for ephemeral cyber-based material authored by unknown individuals.

In addition to the commercial publications you are likely to find in your law school bookstore, you should be able to find topic-targeted questions by surfing the Internet. New sites pop up each month. Use a powerful search engine and go hunting for those issue-specific questions. Caution: consider the source before relying on the accuracy of any answers you find in cyberspace.

Some of the sites you will find are commercial (with study aids for sale); some are non-profit (law school based, for example); some are offered by students or professors who just want to help. As you tour the web, however, keep in mind:

CALI is a non-profit consortium of law schools that researches and develops computer-mediated legal instruction. Find CALI at http://www.cali.org.

- It is easy to spend far too much time searching for helpful material on the web. Avoid this distraction.
- Just because it appears on your computer monitor, it isn't necessarily reliable. Approach "model answers" with caution, especially those from law students.
- Try to stick with reliable, well-recognized sources. For example, "CALI" (The Center for Computer Assisted Legal Instruction) offers a

broad spectrum of instructional material, quizzes, and innovative methodology. CALI publishes hundreds of computer-based tutorials in dozens of legal subject areas. Many of these tutorials include sample hypothetical questions and explanatory materials to assist students in developing answers.

- Law school exam questions from other law schools are easy to find on the web. The problem is that they have all been designed by professors to be course-specific—you will find that many of them raise problems that are beyond your ken.

Finding practice hypotheticals—enlist the aid of your peers

Perhaps when you were a youngster, you assembled a "plastic man" or "plastic woman" and learned the relative positions and basic functions of the liver, kidney, lungs and heart. In Literature class, you may have been asked to write some verse in iambic pentameter. These are examples of learning about the end product by engaging in construction of a similar product. You and your classmates can develop a deeper understanding of the elements and nuances of a law school examination question by constructing some of your own. You will discover that exam question development is not an easy process. Think about it—given a common law principle such as "Battery is the intentional harmful or offensive touching of one person by another"—how can you put together a very short story which would subtly provide a basis for both the plaintiff and the defendant in a case of alleged battery to convince a judge of the correctness of their positions? To do so requires you to think "backwards" or "constructively"—the converse of *answering* the questions posed by your professor, which requires "deconstructive" analysis. That is, a law school hypothetical examination question sets forth a string of facts which you will need to separate into elemental, legally cognizable categories, analyze in terms of the common law (or a statute or precedential holding), then reassemble as part of a cogent argument. Often, you will be expected to demonstrate the argument supporting "the other side," then explain why yours would prevail in court.

If you and one or more classmates engage in the regular practice of developing and exchanging single-issue hypotheticals, you will immediately begin to grow in your appreciation for the subtle distinctions and hidden theories lurking within a few lines of narrative text. Grappling with question construction, answering questions provided by your most competent peers, and discussing the answers sharpens the analytical skills you need to achieve your objective.

Finding practice hypotheticals—build them yourself

After a few classes in each subject, you will catch on to your professor's method of inventing and continually modifying hypotheticals raised in class. Emulate that style. Write your own hypotheticals. When you do so, include settings, characters, and situations that have personal significance to you. Instead of writing a vignette starring a young boy, who pulls a lawn chair out from under an old woman who is about to sit down at the picnic,[41] create a story about your devilish young cousin, deftly removing your Aunt Elma's rocking chair as she is about to sit down in your living room to watch the second half of the Super Bowl. Your mind is able to construct a much more vivid picture of scenes and people familiar to you, and the "abstractness" of the law dissolves a bit as you apply it to circumstances which have personal meaning and significance to you. Engaging in both the "constructive" and "deconstructive" processes exercises and stretches your mind in a different and rewarding way.

What to do with the practice hypotheticals

The questions you will find on your examinations will vary in type and style from course to course, from professor to professor, and from semester to semester. The type of question most students encounter most often in the first year of law school is the multiple issue essay question. The professor will create a narrative, a brief story, and ask the students to resolve conflicts the factual story raises. To attempt to describe an essay exam in much more detail would be futile, in that there are so many variations. Some include very short factual statements, of two to several sentences; others are pages long. Some raise few issues; others raise an abundance of issues (often an *over*abundance).

Generally, the professor does not identify the legal issue, leaving the students to harvest the facts for those particulars that give rise to problems that may be resolved by applying common law rules, statutes, or some other recognized legal principles. Also, generally, the professor does not specify the rules, statutes, or principles which will lead to resolution—instead, she expects the student to be able not only to determine which rules apply but also to state the rules with clarity and precision. Most importantly, your professor expects each student to explain concisely and cogently how the applicable law can resolve the problems. Usually, excellent explanations will include the defusing of counterarguments, and discussions of how the resolution is consistent with an underlying or overriding policy.

Another way of looking at examination questions, and their inherent challenges to students, is to glance momentarily at what the professors are looking for in student answers. Law professors scrutinize each answer for manifestations of:

- Lawyerly skill in extricating the salient facts from inert, non-determinative facts presented in the narrative.
- Capability to identify and specify the legal issues these key facts raise.
- Ability to recall and accurately set out the applicable law or principle which leads to the resolution of the conflict.
- Logical, organized interweaving of the facts with the elements of the law in a compelling analytical presentation.
- Recognition of the driving policies and purposes of the law in question, and the ability to express how these policies and purposes support the resolution proposed by the answer.
- Proficiency in clear, concise, organized legal writing.

Therefore, each time you approach a practice hypothetical, you should do so with the objective of improving on each of those six criteria.

Keep in mind that as you practice answering exam questions throughout the semester, you are serving three major purposes. You are practicing for the examination, thus assuring yourself of a higher grade than you would achieve with no practice; you are practicing the very skills essential to pass the bar examination on the first attempt; and you are practicing law. In other words, you are doing the very thing that most lawyers do constantly in their professional careers (distillation of legal issues from jumbled facts, recollection of the laws and principles that apply to those issues, and composition of concise and cogent written legal analyses).

How do you go about preparing a written answer to a hypothetical? Initially, you should be practicing on self-selected issue-specific short questions of two to several sentences in length. Accordingly, the legal issue that is raised by the facts should not be much of a mystery to you. Nor should the rule (applicable law) be hidden from you. Your most significant chore as a novice in this practice will be to learn how to state the argument that leads to the conclusion you argue for.

In its most simple form, a succinct law exam answer is syllogistic in logical nature. Perhaps you encountered the following example of a syllogism in an undergraduate philosophy course:

- All men are mortal.
- Socrates is a man.
- Therefore, Socrates is mortal.

Or, if you attended a less classically oriented school:

- All cows eat grass.
- Mable is a cow.
- Therefore, Mable eats grass.

Certainly, legal reasoning is much more sophisticated than these simple syllogisms; but comprehending the task of legal reasoning at a most basic level is essential to building up to higher levels. In the context of a law school examination answer, the syllogistic format may play out like this:

- A threat (to injure) may constitute an "act of restraint" essential to establish a claim of "false imprisonment."
- Harvey's statement, "I'm going to stab you if you attempt to leave the room" was a threat (to injure).
- Therefore, Harvey's statement may constitute an "act of restraint" essential to establish a claim of "false imprisonment."

Notice that the first line of the argument, "A threat (to injure) may constitute an 'act of restraint' essential to establish a claim of 'false imprisonment,'" is a statement of a legal rule. Notice, also, that the second line, "Harvey's statement, 'I'm going to stab you if you attempt to leave the room' was a threat (to injure)," interweaves the facts of a hypothetical narration into the logical presentation. The third line is a conclusion, based on application of the fact (Harvey's threatening statement) with the applicable law (that a threat may constitute an act of restraint).

Although the logical format of this three-line presentation is admirable, it would not suffice as an exemplary answer to an examination question for one simple reason: the most important part of the answer is missing. The most important part is this: an explanation of *why* Harvey's threat will or will not be considered forceful enough (or ominous enough) to qualify as an act of restraint. What is it about the threat proffered by this defendant (Harvey) that allows us to determine whether it constitutes an "act of restraint?" How much restraint is required as an element of the tort known as false imprisonment, and why?

Law examination answers that do not supply the explanatory information detailing how each step of the argument is arrived at are said to be "conclusory." That is, they recite conclusions without stating supportive analysis. A display of the thought process leading to every conclusion is essential in a law examination answer. When you enter the professional practice, judges, lawyers, and clients will be asking, "How did you reach that conclusion?" Throughout law school, your professors

For an in-depth "nuts and bolts" description of how to answer a law school hypothetical, eventually turn to Part Four, "Hitting the Target: Scoring High on Law School Exams."

In the false imprisonment example above, if the student were to write simply, "Harvey's threat constituted an act of restraint sufficient to support plaintiff's claim of false imprisonment," that statement, without further explanation would be "conclusory."

will expect you to respond to that latent question in every class session and on every examination. The ability to *conclude* is not what "thinking like a lawyer" is about—rather, you are developing the ability to *persuade* another that the conclusion you have reached is supportable by application of rules of law to a set of facts. Practice *that* when you answer practice hypotheticals.

Critiquing your answers to practice hypotheticals

You need to critique the answers you write to hypotheticals. Different commercial sources for the *questions* will provide different explanations of what should be included in your *answers*. For example, the *First Year Questions & Answers* book (Emanuel's publication) provides very good—but very bare bones—answers. Most professors are looking for more extensive analysis and discussion than this book provides. On the other hand, the *Examples & Explanations* series (published by Aspen) tends to provide "explanations" which resemble discussions or one-sided conversations more than law school exam answers. If a professor provides sample hypotheticals for you, more often than not the closest you will see to a sample answer will be a list of issues, and perhaps some questions that should have crossed your mind while answering.

| Each of these commercial study aids is described near the end of this book. |

When you answer an examination question, you should interweave facts, law and policy considerations into a series of cogent, compelling arguments. Your professors expect accurate statements of the law and well-organized presentation of legal discourse.

As you answer practice hypotheticals, then check your answers against a prewritten source, you may notice that some of the issues, definitions, rules of law, or policy considerations may not have been as fresh in your mind as you would like. Don't *worry* about that. That's right—don't *worry*. But fix it. Your objective is to walk into that final examination room filled with well-deserved self-confidence. If you are working well in advance of the examination period, you have enough time to remedy the problem—"worry" is unproductive.

Your goal should be *fluency in the language of the law*—you should be fully prepared to "spot," identify, and discuss every issue you have covered in class. You should be fully prepared to resolve hypothetical problems as lawyers do, displaying this resolution in strong, lucid, persuasive writing. This fluency comes from practice. Continue to practice answering hypothetical questions in writing.

Keep in mind that, although "issue-spotting" is an important aspect of exam answering, nevertheless, it is but *one* aspect. Rich, deep, insightful, comprehensive, persuasive, thoughtful *analysis* is what professors are looking for. In that sense, there is often no "correct" answer to any question—there are superior answers and inferior answers. On the other hand, failure to spot a significant issue in a hypothetical containing a paucity of issues, may lead to a disappointing exam grade.

To obtain the greatest benefit from the experience of answering hypotheticals, especially time-constrained simulated examination sessions, you should evaluate and critique your answers. Ask your fellow students to swap practice exam answers with you, so you can benefit from critical comments of others. Ask the following questions during your evaluation process.

Issue: Did I correctly identify the issues?
- Did I address the precise question(s) the professor asked?
- Were all the relevant issues identified?
- Were non-issues identified and dismissed?

Rule: Did I write or paraphrase the appropriate rules of law?
- Did I include rules in the answer?
- Were the rules appropriate to include?
- Were the rules correctly stated?

Analysis: Did I interweave the salient facts with the applicable law and appropriate policy considerations?
- Was the answer *conclusory*?
- Did the answer include all (and only) the legally significant facts?
- Where necessary, did I include counterarguments?
- Where applicable, did I include policy considerations?
- Did I use policy to resolve a rules conflict, to break a "tie" in the facts, or to explain the conclusion(s)?
- Did I discuss the reasoning of prior decisions and consider how such reasoning would impact the decision in the hypothetical?

Judgment: Did I exhibit good judgment in time allocation for each issue?
- Did I raise and dismiss those issues that did not need further discussion?
- Did I discuss in depth those issues that required detailed analysis?

Structure: Did I organize the issues in a logical manner?
- Was there an identifiable organization, or did I take a shotgun approach?
- Did I discuss issues in related clusters?
- Did I employ a readable organizational structure to present and discuss each issue?

Conclusion: Did I arrive at a well-reasoned and well-explained conclusion?
- Did the answer have a "bottom line" or did I end with an equivocal, "this is a question the jury will have to decide" statement?
- Was the conclusion adequately explained?
- Was the conclusion a surprise, or did it logically follow from the analysis?
- Did my conclusion answer the question posed by the exam?

Style: Did I employ a reader-friendly writing style?
- Was the writing legible?
- Did I paragraph often?
- Did I introduce each paragraph with a topic designation, by subheading and/or topic sentence?
- Was the incidence of grammatical and/or spelling errors minimal?
- Did I properly use helpful signposts, transition words and connectives (*since, when, because, thus, therefore, on the other hand,* etc.)?

Then follow with this very important step: Make a list of what you plan to do differently when you take an actual final exam. For example, consider:
- Did you miss one or more of the issues entirely? How do you plan to assure yourself that will never happen again?
- Did you waste valuable time restating (or repeating) the facts given in the problem, rather than focusing on the analysis of the issues presented by these facts?
- Were your discussions of the various issues as detailed as necessary to demonstrate adequately that you can pinpoint issues, that you know the law, and that you are able to engage in high-level legal analysis? Did you discuss policy? Did you present alternatives and counter-arguments?
- Did you become sidetracked on issues that weren't actually raised by the fact patterns?
- Was your organization clear and coherent, or did you skip from issue to issue and back again, repeating some points and missing others?

If your answer seemed to have one or more of these problems, consider the variety of possible corrective actions you may take. You may wish to add detail to your course summarizing process (including more factual detail from the cases) making sure that you see how the cases illuminate the general doctrines. Such a detailed course summary (and understanding that comes from the *production* of the summary) is crucial in eliminating many of these exam-answering problems.

Or were your problems mainly due to organization and strategy during the exam? If this is the case, then your summarizing might be fine, but your exam-taking strategy—including time allocation—might need some work. Rethink; then practice!

This seventh Component of Assessment Targeted Study, repeated practice at answering hypothetical questions—"rehearsal"—is essential to working at your highest level when it counts the most: on the final exam. As you become more *pro*ficient and more *e*fficient at the first several components, more of your study time should become available to engage in answering practice hypotheticals in writing. Just how do you allocate your time to accomplish this objective? Discover the answer to that question in Part III, "Time Management and Resource Allocation."

---

[7] Philip C. Kissam, *Law School Examinations*, 42 Vand. L. Rev. 433, 458 (1989).

[8] James E. Moliterno & Fredric I. Lederer, *An Introduction to Law, Law Study, and the Lawyer's Role* 58 (Carolina Academic Press 1991)

[9] Paul Bateman, *Ten Instructions for Briefing Cases*, available at http://www.swlaw.edu/g/briefingcases.html (1999)

[10] Helen Shapo & Marshall Shapo, *Law School Without Fear: Strategies for Success* 17 (Foundation Press 1996).

[11] "SQ3R" was invented during World War II by Francis Robinson, a psychologist, to help military personnel undergoing accelerated university courses. See Francis Pleasant Robinson, *Effective Study* (Harper Collins College Division 1970).

[12] James J. Brosnahan, *Are You Going Trough Life Without a Trial Book?* 502 PLI/Lit 7, 9 (May 5, 1994).

[13] Paul I. Weiner & Charles C. Warner, *Trial Strategy and Preparation in Employment Litigation*, 522 PLI/Lit 283, 288 (Practising Law Institute, June 1955).

[14] Paula Lustbader, *Construction Sites, Building Types, and Bridging Gaps: A Cognitive Theory of the Learning Progression of Law Students*, 33 Willamette L. Rev. 315, 325 n.20 (1997).

[15] Amsterdam & Bruner, *Minding the Law*, 19.

[16] Fischl & Paul, 69.

[17] Daniel S. Kleinberger, *Agency, Partnerships, and LLCs* xxiv (Aspen Law & Business 2002).

[18] Fischl & Paul, 68.

[19] U.S. Constitution, preamble.

[20] Carolyn J. Nygren, *Starting Off Right in Law School* 93 (Carolina Academic Press 1997).

[21] Paul D. Supnik, *Flow Charting—A New Graphics Tool for the Lawyer*, Los Angeles Lawyer Magazine (Dec. 1992) *available at* http://www.supnik.com/flow.htm.

[22] Rodney Jew & Martin Q. Peterson, *Envisioning Persuasion: Painting the Picture for the Jury*, Trial Magazine, Oct. 1, 1995, at 74, *available at* 1995 WL 15142749.

[23] Robert Wegner & Norman Epstein, *Presentation of Opening Statement, in California Practice Guide: Civil Trials and Evidence* (2002).

[24] Laurie Zimet, *Basic Litigation; Legal Research and Writing, in Litigation and Administrative Practice Course Handbook Series* 501 PLI/Lit 507, 522–23 (1994). Laurie Zimet directs the academic support program at Hastings College of Law in California.

[25] Jennifer Blakely Dalrymple, *Teaching and Learning Law with Graphic Organizers*, at http://www.loyno.edu/~dciolino/Classes/GraphicOrganizers.htm (last visited July, 2003).

[26] Paul T. Wangerin, *Learning Strategies for Law Students*, 52 Alb. L. Rev. 471, 507 (1988).

[27] *Id.* at 509.

[28] Michael E. Tigar & Jane B. Tigar, *Federal Appeals Jurisdiction and Practice* §1:8 (West Group 3d ed. 1999).

[29] *See* J. Kirkland Grant, *The Bar Examination: Anachronism or Gatekeeper to the Profession*, 70 N.Y. State B.J. 12, 17 (May/June 1998).

[30] John Delaney, *How to Do Your Best on Law School Exams* 24 (John Delaney Publications 1988).

[31] Steve Emanuel, *Criminal Law: Getting Great Grades with Law in a Flash* 12 (Emanuel Law Outlines, Inc. 1996).

[32] *Id.* at 16.

[33] Mary Campbell Gallagher's doctoral degrees include not only her Juris Doctor (Harvard), but also her Ph.D. in linguistics from the University of Illinois.

[34] Mary Campbell Gallagher, *Scoring High on Bar Exam Essays* 53 (Sulzburger & Graham 1996).

[35] *Id.*

[36] Wangerin, 482.

[37] Philip C. Kissam, *Law School Examinations*, 42 Vand. L. Rev. 433, 458 (1989).

[38] Neil C. Blond, *Blond's Torts* 212 (Sulzburger & Graham 3d ed. 1993).

[39] Kissam, 437.

[40] Jeremy Paul, Professor of Law, University of Connecticut and Michael Fischl, Professor of Law and Dean for Student Academic Affairs, University of Miami (http://lawschool .lexis.com/ exams).

[41] *See Garratt v. Dailey*, 46 Wash. 2d 197, 279 P. 2d 1091 (1955), a standard first-week case in Tort classes around the country.

PART THREE

TIME MANAGEMENT AND RESOURCE ALLOCATION

The Relationship of Time to Law Practice

"Counsel," the judge intoned, *"to begin this morning, I'd like to continue from where we left off yesterday."* Peering over the tops of her wire-rimmed reading glasses, Judge Husereau reminded defense attorney Paul Schultz of someone from his past, but he just couldn't dredge up that memory.

The gray-haired judge continued, "Toward the end of the afternoon, gentlemen, I mentioned that plaintiff's summary judgment motion would stand or fall on the case handed down by our state Supreme Court just last month, Bradley v. Manente.*" As the judge spoke, the clerk handed her a photocopy of the appellate opinion in that case, which Her Honor quickly flipped through, scanning several passages she had highlighted late last night. "Mr. Schultz, since your client has the most to lose if I grant this motion, perhaps you'd like to begin. Just how does the* Bradley *decision affect your position?"*

As Paul rose to address the court, Maria, his client, shifted in her seat. Paul's assurances of an "air-tight case" only last week had bolstered her confidence. Although the thousand dollar check Maria de la Cruz had delivered to Paul's office that day had nearly depleted her savings, it was worth every penny to keep her job as a preschool teacher. The school district's termination of her contract was unwarranted, unfair, and—as attorney Schultz had advised her—"patently illegal." She had a lot riding on this case, and on this morning's hearing in particular—her career, her income, her self-respect.

"Your Honor," Paul Schultz began slowly—Maria noticed a disturbing hesitancy in his voice—"I'm afraid I was unable to read that case last night. You see, last night was my wedding anniversary. Denise and I always spend the night at the Norwich Inn on our anniversary. Under the circumstances, I didn't have time to thoroughly prepare for this morning's hearing." Paul shuffled his feet as he looked over at the court reporter, who glared at him unmercifully.

Maria, horrified, listened as Judge Husereau said brusquely, "Well, counsel, that makes my job much easier. I did read the Bradley *case, and it seems to me as though it works to the school district's advantage. Unfortunately for your client, without hearing her side of the argument, I'm bound to rule in favor of the school district. Accordingly, Ms. de la Cruz's defense, based on her claim that the district's action is illegal under the Education Act, is hereby stricken."*

"But Your Honor," Paul pleaded as the Judge stood and turned to exit the bench, "If we could just recess for half an hour, to give me time to ..."

*"You've had your time, Mr. Schultz, and you didn't use it to prepare, apparently. I've made my ruling. This hearing is over. Good day, sir."
The old memory popped into Paul's consciousness now. The frown on Judge Husereau's face was nearly identical to the frosty scowl of a law professor he endured during his first year at Barrister Law School. Paul flashed on memories of several episodes, now combined into one unpleasant snapshot, of his feeling of panic and (as he told his friends afterwards) intimidation when he was called upon—underprepared—in class. It all came back to him now—he felt sick to his stomach.*

"I'm sorry, Maria," he explained—lamely—in the baroque corridor outside the quaint courtroom. "I really didn't realize how important that case would be to ours. Don't worry, I'll file a motion for reconsideration right away."

"Paul," Maria whispered, as tears streamed down her face, "You don't understand. I'm out of money and out of time. I'll just have to forget teaching. I need to look for some other job—I need to feed my children. Goodbye, Paul." Maria turned slowly, her head bowed. Crestfallen, she walked out the courthouse exit.

"A lawyer's time is his stock in trade." Abraham Lincoln aptly characterized the importance of time in the practice of law.

Most lawyers have more work than time to complete it, and nearly every endeavor is constrained by temporal parameters which too often seem too stringent—thus, the essential importance of exquisite management of this precious resource. Not only does the practicing lawyer need to complete her work efficiently and effectively, but she also *must* balance the personal aspects of her life: spiritual, physical, familial and intellectual. If she loses touch with her inner being, substantially reduces her exercise regimen, spends too little time with her children, and never reads Shakespeare, she ceases to work at optimum levels, and the entire enterprise suffers. Why bother?

*Achieving balance is a practice. It's a challenge and a necessity. When you are out of balance—that is, when you give significantly more attention to one part of yourself than to others—you feel it....
[Y]ou may find yourself trying to believe that your success in one area—your work, for example—compensates for your lack of attention to other areas, say, your relationships or your physical and emotional health. And likely as not, you will come to feel less effective in every part of your life, even the one that claims most of your energy. Practicing balance, like practicing law, is an ongoing affair. ... You keep practicing.*[42]

Apparently our sixteenth president knew no female attorneys, not unusual in the nineteenth century. The phrase "stock in trade" refers to the merchandise on the shelf of the general store—the inventory.

Even as Professor Corinne Cooper exhorts her students to "Work! Work!" more than they are accustomed to, she also reminds them "that this is the beginning of the delicate balancing act they will perform for the rest of their professional lives. Developing good habits is a part of your professional training." Accordingly, she counsels them to plan time for healthy eating, sleeping, relaxing activity, and engagement with family members and friends. Balance is the key word. Corinne Cooper, *Letter to a Young Law Student*, 35 Tulsa L.J. 275, 293 (2000).

Active, hands-on management and control of one's time is a vital lawyering skill. It is also a vital skill for success in law school.

Nineteenth century philosopher Arthur Schopenhauer suggested, "Ordinary people think merely how they will *spend* their time—a person of intellect tries to *use* it."[43] Lawyers are not ordinary people—they possess and employ exercised intellects, and intellectual exercise takes time. Time is often spoken of in these dry, intellectual, managerial terms, isn't it? Far more elegantly, Argentinean author Jorge Luis Borges put it this way: "Time is the substance from which I am made. Time is a river which carries me along, but I am the river; it is a tiger that devours me, but I am the tiger; it is a fire that consumes me, but I am the fire."[44] Commit to being the river, the tiger, and the fire—commit to *managing* your time, not just to spending it. *Control* how you use your time, don't *be* controlled.

Nuts and Bolts:
Creation of Your FLEX-TRAC
(Flexible Time Resource Allocation Chart)

The higher orders of thinking associated with lawyering demand focus and concentration. To achieve the life/time balance essential for maximum focus and concentration, law students and lawyers need to exercise their executive management capabilities to the utmost. This means aggressive assertion of total control over your most personal resource—your lifetime. How will you "spend" your life?

You have committed to "spend" quite a bit of your lifetime engaging in the practice of law—particularly the next few years. When you realized that you wanted to become a lawyer, you set that as a goal, then signed up for a three-year commitment. When you did that, you exercised macro-control over your "life-time."

The next step is to micro-manage the "spending" of your semesters, months, weeks, and hours—so that you obtain the best return on the expenditure of the next 1000 days of your lifetime.

Time management includes self-control and budgeting

> "[R]esearch shows that more time spent studying does not necessarily result in good grades. In short, students who get good grades do not necessarily study more than students who get lower grades. Second, research shows that students who carefully prepare written schedules of their time, and who then conscientiously stick to those schedules, study much more efficiently than students who study with a catch-as-catch-can approach. Not surprisingly, these students also seem to get better grades."
> Wangerin, 492.

Unlike a financial budget, a time budget allows for no significant deficit spending. You can borrow $100,000 to get through law school, but you can't borrow 100 hours to prepare for your Torts exam. In a few years, you can tap a line of credit, or get a cash advance to cover a lean income quarter, but you can't put off the criminal trial date or explain to your client that his adoption will just have to wait for a few months. Active management of your time, therefore, requires far more self-control than management of your financial affairs.

Management of time requires budgeting of time and is based on two simple premises:

1. All objective-targeted time management begins with planning expenditures of time *in advance*.
2. You can only spend what you have.

What do you have, and how much of it is reasonable to spend? The answer to the first question is easy. Time, the "great equalizer," is the only commodity common to all mankind. Each of us has precisely 24 hours (1440 minutes) in each day and 168 hours (10,080 minutes) in each week.

The answer to the second question—how much time is reasonable to spend?—is objective-dependent. You alone can determine how much of your time is reasonable to spend on each objective, given your special circumstances of family obligations, health concerns, and other extracurricular pursuits. Nevertheless, some guidelines may help.

Most new bar admitees work long hours. Consider this as a "light" schedule for a typical first- or second-year associate at a law firm:

Monday through Friday	7:30 to 5:30, with a half-hour lunch break
Two nights each week	6:00 to 10:00
Saturday	8:30 to 1:00

> Time management is a vital *life* skill. "Life = time," Alan Lakein writes, "waste your time and waste your life, or master your time and master your life."

That adds up to 60 hours each week. The fortunate associate who works this little enjoys three nights of leisure each week, and most of her weekends free. If she wants to go away for the weekend, she can schedule those weekend hours during the week. Talk about your "dream job"! Employing a similar schedule, the law student carrying 15 credit hours would spend approximately 15 hours in class, and 45 hours each week "practicing" outside of class, studying. This works out just fine, since many law professors generally suggest spending no less than three hours of outside-of-class study time for every classroom hour. For example, at Indiana University School of Law, "the faculty recommends a minimum of three hours of preparation time for each hour of class time."[45]

The law student who understands that she begins the practice of law the day she begins law school should have no difficulty committing to a workweek similar to what she should anticipate after bar admission. Just as many lawyers spend considerably more time at the practice than outlined above; so also do many students. Commit now.

The luxury afforded by law school (as opposed to most law firms, corporate legal departments, law clinics, courthouses, and government agencies) is this: with the exception of 15 classroom hours per week (9 percent of your weekly time cache of 168 hours), you may work whenever and wherever you like. You can adjust your schedule to fit your lifestyle and study preferences, your most effective daily rhythmic activity cycle, and your social/familial obligations.

The *budget* part you can do on paper—just as with financial budgeting; the *self-control* part is the tougher aspect of time management. In order to maximize the amount of control you exercise over your career and life, you need to add healthy doses of passion (boundless enthusiasm), tenacity (determined persistence) and vision (intelligent foresight). Be advised: law students report that, from time to time, passion, tenacity, and vision all wane—sometimes simultaneously. Keep at it.

What about the "Get a Life!" comments you may have heard, thought, and perhaps uttered—all related to someone who seems to spend quite a bit of time involved in a singular endeavor. Consider this: once you commit to the practice of law, it *becomes* (a most essential part of) your life. As soon as you commit to practicing law—whether in law school or later, you will have *gotten* a life. Also, do the math: If you sleep eight hours nightly, and focus on law school for 60 hours weekly, you will have more than *50 hours each week* to attend to the other parts of your life: family life, spiritual activity, exercise, eating, socializing, and household chores, for example. It's about balance.

How to manage your time in law school

To maximize your lifetime, to obtain the most reward for your expenditure, follow these four steps (detailed below):

1. Establish precise quantifiable objectives.
2. Divide each objective into components.
3. Design the critical path.
4. Allocate time in writing.

Step One—Establish precise quantifiable objectives

Major league baseball pitchers focus on the center point of a 14-inch leather disc (called a catcher's mitt) as they rocket their 97 miles-per-hour fastballs 60.5 feet toward hopeful batters. Archers focus on a one-inch black disc (called a bull's-eye) 50 meters away. Ski racers envision an imaginary path that a free-falling object would travel down the race course (called the "fall line"), and then stay as close to that line as the course markers allow.

Successful lawyers and law students focus on objectives, too—precise, *quantifiable* objectives. Just as the pitcher has his long-range goal of a nine-inning shutout victory, his mid-range goal of a "three-up-three-down" first inning, and a 75 m.p.h. changeup low and outside for the first pitch, each of the other sports professionals can articulate their precise quantifiable goals. So can many lawyers, and so do law students who are striving for their personal bests while practicing law in law school.

Not every law student is gunning for that valedictory position, the top ten percent (class rank), or even the dean's honor list. Because of family or financial obligation, business or social interests, or other motivating

Passion—"It's easy to say 'no!' when there's a deeper 'yes!' burning inside. (Stephen R. Covey) Wilbur Wright spoke of the Wright Brothers' passion to fly: "We could hardly wait to get up in the morning."

Tenacity—"By gnawing through a dike," Edmund Burke pointed out, "even a rat may drown a nation." "Law school is like wrestling a gorilla. You don't quit when *you* get tired—you quit when the *gorilla* gets tired." (Robert Strauss)

Vision—"The great thing in the world is not so much where we stand, as in what direction we are moving." (Oliver Wendell Holmes) Peter Schultz thinks of it this way: "Three people were at work on a construction site. All were doing the same job, but when each was asked what the job was, the answers varied. 'Breaking rocks,' the first replied. 'Earning my living,' the second said. 'Building a cathedral,' said the third.

factors, many students are content to fill out the lower three quartiles of the class roster. Perhaps surprisingly, many of these students experience as much or more stress and anxiety than those to whom top grades are a priority. The reason is clear in many cases: they convince themselves that they are in *school*—a familiar and rather comfortable place for these gifted college graduates to be—then, within weeks, they realize that they have misjudged their situation. They are awash in conflicting doctrines, flooded with unintelligible foreign sounding language, inundated with confusing sets of rules and split hairs—they claim they are drowning. They are right. They have grossly miscalculated. Here's what they haven't done: these students, believing mid-range grades will come easily, have neglected to establish precise, quantifiable objectives.

In other words, whether your objective is to ace the Torts class, or merely pass, you will substantially increase your chance of hitting your target cleanly and efficiently if you identify it with specificity.

Career objectives often shift during law school. The student who enters with the idea of moving from the graduation stage to the FBI Training Academy in Virginia may decide—after a semester in the school's legal clinic—to spend the first few years of her career representing abused children. The student who begins law school with the intention to return to the family-operated business to work in the general counsel's office may be unable to resist the lure of a prosecutorial calling. The student who enters with no specific career goal may realize after several months that she desperately wants to clerk for (or become) an appellate justice.

For many positions, good grades are an entrée; for many positions, poor grades are a bar to entry. Aim high, and keep as many options as possible open during your first few semesters. But keep in mind—it's not all about grades. It's about preparing yourself for the professional practice of law. Not coincidentally, the most effective preparation for professional practice is precisely the same as the best preparation for exams (usually the sole determiners of grades).

Therefore, if you truly aim to be the best lawyer you can be, aren't you aiming for the best grades you can achieve?

Aim high.

Example: Precise quantifiable objective for Torts—"A"

Step Two—Divide each objective into components

The tennis player aiming to rise from beginner to tournament champion may divide her tennis-playing objective into several general components, for example:

> How does participation in student organizations relate to your law school objectives? Legal fraternities, student bar organizations, clubs based on interests and backgrounds, the school newspaper, public interest law student groups—you will be solicited by many of these to join as early as orientation week. Socializing and working for social concerns while in law school may be very appealing and important—however, prioritizing is essential. Thoughtfully consider the time impact and be prepared to postpone active participation until after the first semester or first year.

- Offense.
- Defense.
- Conditioning for strength.
- Conditioning for stamina.
- Nutrition.

She'd then segment these general areas; for example, offense might include:

- The serve.
- The lob.
- The volley.
- The backhand.
- The overhead.

<table>
<tr><td>

Remember that the *quantity* of time is only part of the story—hands-on micro-management of the time is essential. Professor Wangerin insists that time and effort management is "the most basic studying skill ... the foundation for all the rest." Wangerin, 491.

</td><td>

For each of these sub-disciplines, she'll construct a training/conditioning program designed to provide near daily practice of each.

Likewise, the law student should divide each course objective into several components, then construct a program designed to provide near daily practice of each. For example, to score your personal best on the Torts exam, you will need to demonstrate these abilities:

</td></tr>
</table>

- Issue identification—discern the subtle legal issues raised within a factual narrative.
- Statement of law—precisely state the pertinent rules of law, definitions, corollaries, and exceptions attendant to each issue identified.
- Analytical writing—write a cogent analysis of the problems arising from the interplay of the facts and the laws with underlying policies, principles, and moral considerations.
- Logical, persuasive writing—present fluent, persuasive written explanations or arguments resolving the factual and legal conflicts and quandaries.

The Law CATS are described in detail throughout Part Two.

To achieve mastery in these four aspects—with your target being to score your personal best on the final examination—turn to the CATS. The Components of Assessment Targeted Study for your Torts class include:

- Read and brief (the SQ3R method adapted to law study).
- Actively attend every class and take notes.
- Transform your notes.
- Prepare course summaries.
- Develop flow charts.
- Internalize (learn by heart—commit to memory).
- Practice answering hypotheticals in writing.

Of course a less doctrinally focused course, such as Legal Research and Writing, will require a different set of components.

Step Three—Design your critical path

"Critical path" is a term used by construction project supervisors as they establish the schedule of design production, material ordering and delivery, inspections, equipment needs, labor requirements, and all the myriad of activities essential to complete a major work of construction. They do not want the concrete foundation poured and hardened before the plumbing inspector approves the waste drainage system (which the concrete will cover). They do not want carpenters standing around all morning waiting for the nail delivery truck.

To design the critical path for your Torts course, you should gather information from four sources:

1. *The course syllabus.* All syllabi differ. Some are vague, others quite precise. Some demonstrate flexibility, others rigidity. Most are designed to communicate the course objectives, reading schedule, examination date(s), and assignment dates (if any). Your ultimate target date is usually disclosed on the syllabus: the date of the final examination. Note this, along with any other assessment events (papers or midterm examinations).

> Caveat: Some professors alter the schedule as the course progresses. Take this into consideration when planning.

2. *Your professor.* Your professor will offer sound advice about how to do well in her class. Some of that advice will include announcements of review sessions and other opportunities to learn more about how to excel. Some professors place course objectives and expectations online —this text has been carefully crafted to inure to your academic benefit. Read it. On the other hand, don't expect every professor to provide a clear roadmap to excellence. Many believe law students should draw their own maps.

> Even if mid-term exams are ungraded, approach them like the "real thing." These are essential "dry runs."

3. *Your colleagues.* Notice the use of the word "colleagues" instead of "peers." A colleague is a law student; a peer is a student in your class. Find out who fared well in your professor's class *last* year, and ask questions about the professor's methodology and expectations. Does she stick to the schedule on the syllabus? Were her exam tips in class predictive of what appeared on the exam? If a student brings her an answer to a practice exam, will she discuss it and offer advice?

4. *Your Academic Support office.* Many Academic Support professionals in law schools know the answers to most of the professor-specific questions you will need answered in order to produce an effective critical path design. For example, they may be able to tell you where to find recent final or midterm exams your professor has given. They will tell you about whether she sticks to her syllabus or deviates. Some Academic Support personnel have actually attended classes taught by your professor, and they will be able to fully acquaint you with the method and extent of that professor's dispensation of the examination tips and clues. They are also able to inform you of essential special events hosted or promoted by the

Academic Support program, such as simulated exams, course-specific reviews, and exam-answering workshops. Further, many academic support offices offer feedback on students' early efforts at exam answering.

Once you have assembled the necessary information, design the critical path. Here are a few things to keep in mind:

> Study groups can be energizing or enervating, dynamic or distracting. See the supplement "Powerful Study Groups" toward the end of this book.

- During the first semester of law school, you do not have enough perspective or information to begin preparation of course summaries until after three or four weeks.
- Study groups are effective tools but should be spaced according to their objectives (for example, class preparation, exam preparation) and must be used to augment your private study, never to replace it.
- Course summaries should be completed in all courses long before reading week—more than two weeks before finals. This allows you to spend your time just before exams focusing specifically on examination preparation, rather than on learning new material.

> You will meet second- and third-year students who will tell you to wait until the last few days before exams to *begin* "outlining." Ask them if they've ever heard this word: *influenza*. Why wait? Be prepared.

- You should prepare for a midterm as if it is a final, to get the most out of the exercise.
- Plan on attending as many simulated exam sessions as your school offers—these are invaluable dress rehearsals for the real thing.
- Check your school's calendar to find out exactly which days are school holidays. Plan your travel, if any, way in advance to fit in your critical path. A long Thanksgiving weekend with your family, a thousand miles from law school, should provide you with an opportunity for essential relaxation—not frenzy and stress.

Your basic critical path will include all of your courses, running simultaneously. The paths for each subject will be similar, but may differ because of different course requirements, schedules and expectations. After you assemble all the relevant dates, chart out the semester by writing the fixed dates on a semester-long timeline, then adding your preparation essentials.

Here's an example for a Torts class:

> Include all the dates pertinent to *each class*. Include all Legal Writing assignments and draft due dates.

Relevant dates:

August 25	First day of class
October 10	Academic Support exam answering workshop
November 3	In-class midterm (2 hours, closed-book)
November 14	Academic Support simulated exam (3 hours)
November 25	Last day of class
November 21–30	Thanksgiving vacation
December 10	Torts final exam (3 hours, closed book)

You will certainly have many more dates. Add the date you *leave* for Thanksgiving vacation, and the day you *return*; include Mom's visit, and the ski weekend you've planned.

Step Four—Allocate time in writing

Commit to a well-planned, flexible time budget. Consider developing a FLEX-TRAC. The FLEX-TRAC (<u>Fl</u>exible <u>T</u>ime <u>R</u>esource <u>A</u>llocation <u>C</u>hart) empowers students to take total control of their lives—by weekly planning and employment of high-level executive management strategies. The objective is to construct a useable chart with these criteria:

- A one-week display—for focus.
- Significant size (consider 24 by 30 inches, for placement on your study room wall)—for ease of reading and modification.
- Adjustability—for midweek alteration.
- Formality—for self-imposing the feeling of self-control of your life.

> The FLEX-TRAC system may be simulated on smaller paper or by using a computer program. However, the "bigness" of the FLEX-TRAC provides for many advantages—especially for the visual/kinesthetic learner.

Constructing a FLEX-TRAC

Step One—Draw a seven-day calendar

Use eight columns (the far left column is for the times of day) with eleven rows. Across the top, place the names of the days of the week, beginning with Monday, ending with Sunday.

> See the sample FLEX-TRAC at the end of this section.

Step Two—Label each row with a time "chunk" which relates to your typical weekday and school schedule

For example, if you normally awaken near 6:00 a.m., spend about an hour eating and dressing, a half hour exercising, and a few minutes commuting, your first time label (for the first row of your FLEX-TRAC) may be 6:00–8:30. The next several rows should approximately correspond to your institution's daily schedule (using on-the-hour or half-hour increments). Design your time chunks in 60, 90 or 120-minute increments around that schedule. These blocks of time might read:

> You have just divided the 112 hours of your weekly "awake time" into about 70 segments. Soon, you will allocate about half of those chunks to your career and half to the other essential aspects of your life: your family, your health (physical, mental, spiritual, emotional), and the administrative aspects of daily living.

6:00–8:30
8:30–10:00
10:00–11:00
11:00–12:00
12:00–2:00
2:00–3:00
3:00–5:00

Divide the remaining rows into comfortable evening increments, corresponding to your new life-style and preferences, for example:

5:00–6:00
6:00–7:30
7:30–10:00

Make sure that no time-gaps exist between the rows—the last time in each row label should be the first time in the next row label. The first number in the left-hand column should approximate your generally acceptable waking time, and the last time in that column should correspond to your bedtime.

Step Three—Laminate both sides of your chart

Many local print shops will laminate large sheets for you. You can purchase laminating material at most office supply stores. This allows for you to write on the chart with erasable markers, adjust the times and reallocate to suit your needs, and then re-use the chart each week. This "flexibility" feature is important, for no two weeks will be the same.

Step Four—Write the names of your classes in the corresponding time slots on the chart

Step Five—Determine how you will spend your study time for each subject

This step requires you to consciously determine how much of your limited time you will spend for each subject on each of the Law CATS. For example, a student may decide to divide her Components of Assessment Targeted Study time for the fourth week of Contracts as follows:

- Read and brief—2 hours per class, twice weekly.
- Class attendance and note-taking—(already covered by scheduled class periods).
- Transforming class notes—15 minutes per class session.
- Course summary preparation—2 hours.
- Developing flow chart—1 hour.
- Internalizing—½ hour.
- Answering practice hypotheticals in writing—1½ hours.

Remember to list these components for *each* of your courses. The total time allocated for the Law CATS activities should equal approximately three times the amount of time you spend in class.

> The total study time for this 3-credit class, in this example, is 9½ hours. As the weeks fly by, your time allocations will shift. For example, as your fluency in the language of the law increases, so will your reading and briefing efficiency. Then the time engaged in that component will decrease, allowing for more time to spend on writing your course summaries. Reevaluate your time allocation weekly.

Step Six—Create a "balance" list for weekly "life-essential activities"

List the activities you intend to engage in to balance your life and allocate time for each activity. For example, the balance list of an unmarried jogger who loves to cook and invite friends over, and attend movies or plays on occasion, may include these weekly allocations:

- Jogging: 5 hours.
- Attending church: 2 hours.
- Dining: 8 hours.
- Socializing: 10 hours.
- Running the household: 10 hours.

Another student, a married fellow with two youngsters, may include "family time," and cut "social" back to one hour since he promised his wife that his rugged law school schedule would still allow him to have dinner with his wife and kids and focus on his family often during each week.

Step Seven—Write your Law CATS and life-essential activities on the FLEX-TRAC

Adjust your chart to create a very realistic and "doable" schedule. Try to arrange your 15 hours of class and 45 hours of study so that it approximates a typical attorney work schedule—something like 8:00 to 5:30 five days each week; several evenings a week; and a partial but significant chunk of weekend time.

Strategically place the study chunks where they will integrate best with your class and life schedule. Consider the "critical path" concept as you decide when to perform each activity.

- Read and brief for a class no more than a full day before that class, and never just before the class (in case the assignment takes longer than you anticipate).
- Transform class notes as soon as possible following each class session.
- Work on your flow chart after your course summary is brought up to date.
- Engage in memory work after course summarizing.
- Practicing writing answers to hypothetical essay exam questions should be the last activity of the week's study regimen for each class, if possible.

Avoid scheduling study time when you know it will be most difficult, unproductive, or certain to conflict with your family's schedule. The idea here is for *you* to actively control and manage your time to *your*

> The "household" category is for chores—paying bills, shopping, cleaning, changing spark plugs, laundering the cat, and other essential homemaking activities.

> Results of a survey of first-year students at one law school demonstrated that "only 3% of the law school students were most alert in the early morning, whereas 37% were evening high-energy preferents. Eight percent 'came alive' after 10:30 a.m., but for 57%, afternoon was the best time of day." The authors of the article refer to the peak times as "chronobiological highs." Robin Boyle & Rita Dunn, *Teaching Law Students Through Individual Learning Styles*, 62 Alb. L. Rev. 213, 233–34 (1998).

> Does this seem like too much time? Look at it this way: If you spend 56 hours sleeping, 15 hours in class, and 45 hours studying law ("practicing"), then you have 52 hours each week—(30% more time than most people spend at "full-time" jobs)—to socialize, exercise, groom, eat, attend church, shop, relax, and attend to life's other essential activities.

best advantage, and not to sit back passively and watch the practice of
law gobble up your life. (Highlight that last sentence.)

Those law students who complain that there is not enough time in the
day to finish their work, who tell tales of "all-nighters" and lost
weekends, are students who are failing to manage their time and failing
to control their lives. Be mindful of time each day. Patch any "leaks,"
those unaccounted for minutes and hours that, together, leave law
students with the feeling they do not have enough time in the day to
attend to their priorities. Professor John Kunich of Roger Williams
University School of Law explains:

> *It is tragic how most people fail to think about the tendency for
> time to slip through their grasp—tragic, but not surprising since
> time is invisible and intangible, both omnipresent and impossible
> to capture. But if we do not confront the issue of time leak, we
> leave ourselves vulnerable to running out of it before we even
> know what is happening.*[46]

After allocating your resources, managing your time at the highest
levels of your executive capability, and assiduously practicing each of
the Components of Assessment Targeted Study—you need to demonstrate your proficiency by hitting the target: scoring high on law school
exams. Turn to the next section for the nuts and bolts of how to achieve
that objective.

---

[42] Steven Keeva, *Transforming Practices: Finding Joy and Satisfaction in the Legal Life* 37 (Contemporary Books 1999).

[43] Arthur Schopenhauer, *Aphorisms on the Wisdom of Life.*

[44] Jorge Luis Borges, *Labyrinths,* "A New Refutation of Time" (1964).

[45] See http://www.iulaw.indy.indiana.edu/admiss/lawstudy (July, 2003).

[46] John C. Kunich, J.D., & Richard Lester, Ph.D., *Time Management Techniques for the Survival Leader, in Survival Kit for Leaders* 172 (Skyward Publishing 2003).

Sample Flexible Time-Resource Allocation Chart (FLEX-TRAC)

Your allocation will be different

	MONDAY	TUESDAY	WEDNESDAY	THURSDAY	FRIDAY	SATURDAY	SUNDAY
6:00 to 8:30	TIME FOR A HEALTHY BREAKFAST *and* EXERCISE EVERY DAY OF THE WEEK (Include Commute Time)						
8:30 to 10:00	*TORTS*	*PROPERTY*	*TORTS*	*PROPERTY*	*TORTS*	Create **Torts** Course Summary & Prepare Flow Chart	
10:00 to 11:00	Read & Brief **Property**	Read & Brief **Civil Procedure**	Write Answers to Torts Hypos	Read & Brief **Property**	Write Answers to Torts Hypos		*OTHER PARTS OF LIFE*
11:00 to Noon	*CONTRACTS*		*CONTRACTS*		*CONTRACTS*	Create **Property** Course Summary & Prepare Flow Chart	
Noon to 2:00 (Quick Lunch)	Prepare for **Legal Writing**	Write Answers to CivPro Hypos	Create **Contracts** Course Summary	Read & Brief **Civil Procedure** & Internalize	Create **Contracts** Course Summary & Prepare Flow Chart		
2:00 to 3:00	*LEGAL WRITING*	*CIVIL PROCEDURE*	*LEGAL WRITING*	*CIVIL PROCEDURE*	Write Answers to **Contracts** Hypos	*OTHER PARTS OF LIFE*	
3:00 to 5:00	Read & Brief **Contracts**	Work on **Legal Writing** Assignment	Work on **Legal Writing** Assignment	Write Answers to **Property** Hypos	Create **CivPro** Course Summary & Prepare Flow Chart		
5:00 to 6:00	TIME FOR DINNER WITH FRIENDS *or* FAMILY EVERY DAY OF THE WEEK						
6:00 to 7:30	*OTHER PARTS OF LIFE*	*OTHER PARTS OF LIFE*	*OTHER PARTS OF LIFE*	*OTHER PARTS OF LIFE*	*FRIDAY NIGHT OUT OR WITH FAMILY*	*SATURDAY NIGHT OUT OR WITH FAMILY*	*OTHER PARTS OF LIFE*
7:30 to 10:00	Read & Brief **Property** & Internalize	Read & Brief **Torts** & Internalize	Read & Brief **Property** & Write Hypo Answers	Read & Brief **Torts** & Write Hypo Answers			Read & Brief **Contracts**

SLEEP HOURS 56

CLASS HOURS 15

STUDY HOURS 45

OTHER PARTS OF LIFE HOURS 52

NOTE BALANCE

PART FOUR

HITTING THE TARGET: SCORING HIGH ON LAW SCHOOL EXAMS

The Relationship of Exams to Law Practice

Gleaming brass, polished mahogany, and imported Italian porcelain tile around the perimeter of the carpeted floor—the boardroom at Cypress Bank was built for comfort. Mark eased himself into one of the cream-colored leather chairs and placed his legal pad and fountain pen on the conference table.

"Good morning, Mark." The unmistakable voice of DeWayne Tilton, President of Cypress Bank, filled the room as he entered and greeted the young attorney. Mark Whitlock rose quickly and shook the President's hand. "We're pleased you could join us. The Board members and I have a few 'troubled' construction loan files we need to plow through and make some quick decisions."

"I hope I can be of assistance, Mr. Tilton."

"Call me DeWayne," the silver-haired man insisted. "I'm sure you'll be very helpful. The partners at your firm seemed to think so. That's why you're here today, isn't it? They told me you're the 'go-to' guy when it comes to problem loans."

Mark had just recently joined Hartnett, Lombardi & Longwill after two years in the legal department at a local credit union. The firm had hired him for just this purpose—they hoped he would continue to develop his burgeoning expertise in "loan workouts," the bankers' term for handling problems associated with borrowers defaulting on large commercial loans.

Mr. Tilton introduced the young lawyer to each of the board members as they arrived. Soon, the five women and seven men comprising the Board of Directors all sat at the table. The senior director, Samantha diSalvo, addressed Mark.

"Mr. Whitlock, what I'd like to do is acquaint you with the facts related to each of these loans, and ask you to guide us through an understanding of where the Bank stands vis-à-vis our chances of recovering our investments. The question in each case will be pretty much the same: should we give the borrower more time to financially recover, or should we proceed immediately with litigation? We need to hear from you precisely what the governing law is, how it applies to the circumstances of each loan, and what your recommendation is."

As each file was addressed, Ms. diSalvo distributed a two-page narrative outlining the initial terms of the loan, describing the construction project for which the funds had been lent, and summarizing the current financial situation of the debtor. Mark read through each quickly, circling a few key facts, making some marginal notes, and scratching out a few phrases on his yellow legal pad. Several of the directors acquainted Mark with some of the new bank policies—

including the fact that they needed to make their decisions with one eye on the recent criticism they received from the Federal Bank Examiner's office for some alleged liberality in their treatment of loans made to local contractors.

Mark handled each of the problem files in much the same way—he identified the significant legal issues, explained which banking regulations would apply, then proceeded to discuss the particular facts in light of the applicable regulations. He presented the "pros and cons" of litigation, then concluded with a recommendation which took into account not only the rules but also the bank's fiscal policies and regulatory concerns.

Throughout the morning, one silent Board member smiled inwardly. Stephanie Wilcox, the newest member of the Bank's Board of Directors, was an evening division law student in her second year. She may have been the only person at the table to recognize the structure and style of Mark's well-received responses to each of the loan problems.

The analysis provided by Mark Whitlock was exactly what Stephanie had been practicing since her first days of law school—by writing examination answers. What Mark had done at the meeting orally, Stephanie had learned to do in writing for each exam question: carefully scrutinize the facts, identify the legal issues, articulate the applicable rules of law, interweave the rules with the salient facts, and develop a conclusion consistent with germane policies. Seldom had she seen such a display of cogent, fluent, persuasive analysis. "Mark Whitlock," she silently mused, "You must have been one heck of a law student."

Admission to the bar is admission to a community—a community of practitioners, jurists, clerks, and teachers. The members of this community need to communicate with each other, in order to serve their clients, their employers, their students, and the larger community. In order to do so, they must be capable of fluently articulating legal concepts in the language of the law. Throughout law school, law professors continually assess each student's progress and proficiency—the assessment tools are (usually) law examinations.

Law professors attempt to write examinations that will provide law students with the opportunity to demonstrate their mastery of the subject matter, their fluency in the language of law in general, and a given subject in particular. Exemplary test answers display consummate proficiency in lawyerly thought processes and superlative fluency in the subject matter. A superior test answer will demonstrate a professional facility for critically analyzing complex problems and presenting the analysis—often with a solution—manifesting clarity, comprehension, and marked articulacy in the language of law.

The professors who grade your examination answers are well-equipped to evaluate your skills. Most professors have:

- Excelled as law students, including the writing of superior test answers year after year.
- Demonstrated extraordinary capabilities in analyzing complex legal problems, usually through publication and presentation of scholarly articles and treatises, sometimes also within the professional practice of law.
- Crafted many (often hundreds of) examination questions designed specifically as prompts for displays of lawyerlike reasoning and writing proficiencies.
- Studied, analyzed, and graded hundreds or thousands of law school examinations.
- Reviewed their techniques, grading methods, and grading scales with their colleagues and/or with the institution's Academic Dean.

Law school exams are not graded arbitrarily. Professors who do their jobs well distinguish between an "A minus" answer and a "B plus" answer based on solid criteria and considerable experience. Trust them. Your objective should be to write an answer so solid, so comprehensive, so persuasive, and so elegant, that it will stand out as a nonpareil exemplar of professional lawyerly writing.

The "traditional" type of law school exam most often employed in first-year courses is the blue book exam. That generic term "includes a variety of forms, which can range from one- or two-hour short-answer exams to so-called take-home exams that last five, eight, or ten hours."[47]

Students sometimes ask, "Why must we take exams? Why are we graded at all?" Whether you agree with the justification or not, law school exams (and the grades which are based exclusively upon the results of those exams) serve several functions, which are of considerable importance to law students, law school graduates, law firms, and other employers.

The direct functions of law school examinations are to prepare students to pass state bar examinations and to generate a highly disaggregated class ranking system. Law school grades and class ranks are used to select students for the law school's prestigious extracurricular activities such as law review, moot court programs, and clinic directorships. Most significantly, legal employers use class ranks and law review status to screen and select law students for the more prestigious and lucrative employment opportunities that the legal profession has to offer.[48]

Thus, one relationship between law school exams and law practice is this: how well you do on your exams will most likely have a major impact on whether, when, where, and with whom you practice law, and in what area of law you practice. You may think this is not the case if you plan from the outset of law school to engage in a solo practice or if you are confident of a place in your family's law firm. However, since the economy, your income requirements, your preferences, your perspective, and your sophistication will all be altered significantly during the 1000 days you spend in law school, you may want to keep as many doors open as possible.

Just as importantly, superlative preparation for law school examinations—by attending to the active *practice* of law throughout law school—will prepare you for the *professional* practice of law. She who devotes her time and energy to *practicing* law throughout her law school career by using her time resourcefully and efficiently in pursuit of her triple objective (grades reflective of her high capabilities and hard work, first-time bar exam passage, and successful professional practice) will achieve each of those goals. Isn't that why you are in law school?

Exam Answering: Strategies and Techniques

Nuts & Bolts: Answering Exam Essay Questions

When answering final examination essay questions, students should consider four different aspects:

- Mechanics: the process, the procedures—how to go about answering.
- Logic: organization of each answer to demonstrate a forceful, logical flow toward the conclusion.
- Analysis: the systematic analysis of each area of law.
- Presentation: the best way to display the logical structure of the answer.

The Mechanics

The mechanics of methodically answering a typical law school essay exam question are easily broken down into seven steps. Practice these seven steps as you work throughout the semester (especially toward the end) preparing for finals.

Step One—Start with the "call of the question"

Read the end of the question before you read the beginning or middle. Law school essay exams typically recite a set of facts, then ask for a particular response. For example, after detailing a week-long multi-crime spree by three individuals who may (or not) have conspired with each other, the question may ask, "What crimes, if any did Manny, Mo and Jack commit? Include in your discussion all available defenses." Or, after a vivid description of corporate conniving in a contractual matter, involving activities in several states, the question posed at the end may be, "Assuming the State of Harmony has a 'long-arm' statute, advise Baker Corporation of whether it will be subject to Harmony Superior Court's jurisdiction."

The "call of the question" provides a context for the (often confusing) facts presented in the hypothetical. She who reads the facts with the ultimate problem in mind reads with a subconscious schematic diagram and provides a modicum of order to the streaming narrative of the professor's question. This allows for a sensible basis for step two.

Step Two—Read the entire question from beginning to end and circle the important words

What words are important? You should have an idea of what is important after you know what the ultimate question (the "call" of the question at the end) is. Generally the following items are important:

- Names: you will need to be able to find and identify the parties when you are in a rush during the writing phase of your answering.
- Transactions: every crash, every offer, every sale is important in an exam; do not skim past one by mistake.
- Dates: professors add dates to hypothetical events to alert students to the invocation of some time-related rule.
- Times: whether events took place in the daytime or at night, before or after each other, can be very important.
- Dollar amounts: particularly in Contracts questions, dollar amounts are extremely important to the parties, and they should be to you.
- Quantities: heavy or light, large or small, few or many; all quantities make a difference.
- States: particularly in Civil Procedure questions, the states of residence, of incorporation, of service of process and of filing of the lawsuit are critically important.
- Statutes: often, professors will provide laws, either real or imagined, upon which your answer should be based.
- Adverbs and adjectives: well-crafted questions include modifiers which provide ammunition for arguments; if Joan was "shuffling aimlessly" or "striding purposefully," if Steve was "wandering drunkenly" or "driving cautiously," your answer will differ accordingly.

Step Three—Chart the parties

On a separate sheet of paper, construct a chart—a table, a graphic organizer (flow chart), or even a crude drawing—demonstrating who did what to whom and who is suing whom. Some type of diagram is often essential to keep the parties and their respective claims and defenses straight as you produce your answer. Include abbreviated names, important relationships (spouse, employer, guardian, for example), interactions (who hit whom, who offered what, for example), and which parties are potential plaintiffs and defendants.

Step Four—Make marginal notes as you read the hypothetical a second time

Use abbreviations and "law school shorthand" for this intermediate step. These notes are simply to jog your memory when you get to the next step, to make sure you do not leave out something important.

Step Five—Outline your answer

If any step could be called "most essential," this would be that step. To put the importance of this step into perspective, consider that many law professors suggest that students spend at least one-third of their exam-answering time outlining the answer. Some professors refuse to hand out the bluebooks until more than a third of the time has passed. The style and form of the outline is important only to *you* since you will be graded only on the finished product: the answer as it appears in your bluebook. However, a standard outline approach is to organize the answer according to the various claims that the parties have against each other, and then to include subtopical headings dealing with the various legal issues the question implies you should resolve in your analysis.

> For a one-page question allowing for a 60-minute answer period, a student would be wise to consider spending several minutes on the first four steps, and then spend 15 to 20 minutes outlining her answer.

Step Six—Write the answer

For a one-hour question, the actual time spent writing in the bluebook should be about 30 to 40 minutes (allowing about one-third to one-half of the hour for steps one through five). Of course, since everyone thinks and writes at different speeds, your time may be a bit more or less.

Step Seven—Review your answer

When you read your entire answer, quickly, you should be asking yourself several specific questions: did you respond to the precise call of the question; did you include all the essential elements of a solid answer; should you add anything for clarity or completeness?

The Logic

You need to provide clear, concise, convincing coverage of every issue raised by the hypothetical. After reading your response, your professor must *know* that you thoroughly understand the subject matter. Your answer should be an exemplar of lawyerlike thinking. It must be presented logically.

In order to accomplish a logical presentation of each issue appearing in your answer outline, you need to identify that issue in some way, indicate which rule (or set of rules) a lawyer would employ to resolve the issue, articulate an analysis of how the facts of this hypothetical case are affected by application of the rule, and reason to a solid conclusion.

The steps in the *TICRA-FLIPC* (pronounced *tick—ra—flip—sea*) method will get you off on the right foot. The letters in this acronym stand for:

> You won't find TICRA-FLIPC in other publications. This author invented it. However, you may note that the four letters I-R-A-C are imbedded in this series of ten. Professors across the country complain that the traditional "IRAC" formula taught to many first-year students deceptively over-simplifies the exam-answering process, and woefully misleads students into a shallow, formulaic approach. TICRA-FLIPC is this author's answer to these well-deserved criticisms.

Topic, Issue or Conclusion
… followed by the …
Rule … which leads to the …
Analysis, which is composed of …
Facts and Law Interwoven with Policy, leading to a logical …
Conclusion.

Identification of the Topic, Issue, or Conclusion should precede any discussion. An essay answer should, ideally, flag each separate "issue" by naming it topically ("Res Ipsa Loquitur" or "Negligence Per Se" or "The Last Clear Chance Rule"), or by stating the particular issue ("Whether Jack's violation of the firearms statute constituted negligence per se"), or by stating the conclusion which has yet to be supported ("Jack's firing of the revolver in the crowded saloon constituted negligence per se").

The next step is to identify the rule (meaning, the "rule" of *law*—the common law principle or statute)—often a series of rules—that should be used to resolve the problem. The rule needs to be stated with precision—hence, internalization (memorization if necessary) is essential.

Following identification of the rule that will be employed to resolve the legal problem you have identified, you need to engage in lawyerly "analysis" of the problem. That analysis, in its most fundamental sense, boils down to an interweaving of the facts presented in the hypothetical, with the law you have identified. Often, since reasonable people could view the interplay of the facts and the law somewhat differently, a well-reasoned decision will be driven by the "policy," that is, the underlying reason as to why the rule exists, or how the law should best be used to serve the interests of society. This is the point where you get into the "jurisprudence" aspect of law school. Jurisprudence has to do with "vision" or "insight" into the law, rather than simple mechanical application of the law. Perhaps you recall from as early as your grade school civics class you learned that the legislative branch of a tripartite government *makes* the laws, the executive branch *enforces* the laws, and the judicial branch *interprets* the laws. Welcome to the judicial branch. You are entering a field of interpretation, which calls upon you to engage in a different type of analysis than most people are accustomed to. This is called legal analysis. It is also called "thinking like a lawyer," and that is precisely what your professors expect to see demonstrated in your examination answers.

The last part of each section of your answer should be the conclusion that flows from your analysis—the resolution of the issue expressed or implied at the beginning of the discussion.

Some professors expect quite a bit of policy discussion—indeed, some professors present questions exclusively dedicated to eliciting policy discussions. Others are far less interested in this area of jurisprudence—they focus on issue recognition, statement of law, and legal analysis. As the semester progresses, determine where each of your professors stands along this continuum, by listening during class, by asking second-year students (who have done well in that professor's class), by asking the professor, and by analyzing the professor's past exams.

Three words you will find often in court opinions (which are oftentimes wonderful paradigms for examination answers), used to introduce these very same sections after articulation or identification of the issue to be considered by the court, are "under, here, and therefore." These words are so powerful and ubiquitous (in court opinions) that Dr. Mary Campbell-Gallagher, a nationally reputed bar examination preparation expert, insists that her students use them to introduce the subsections of their bar examination essay answers. Although Dr. Gallagher does not mention the TICRA-FLIPC model, she does suggest that students introduce their *rule* identification with the word "under," their analytical discussion with the word "here," and their conclusion with the word "therefore."[49] Thus:

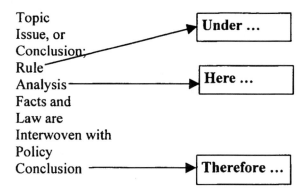

Such a logical layout corresponds to the most basic design of deductive legal reasoning, the syllogism. Syllogistic logical form follows this pattern:

- Major premise: All men are mortal.
- Minor premise: Socrates is a man.
- Conclusion: Therefore, Socrates is mortal.

Similarly, a barebones legal analysis might read:

- Under the common law, a promisee's justifiable detrimental reliance on the promise of another may support a claim of estoppel.
- Here, Sylvia's termination of her lease appears to have been in justifiable detrimental reliance on David's promise.
- Therefore Sylvia's lease termination may support her claim of estoppel.

This is not to imply that the TICRA-FLIPC model is the *only* way to respond to a law school exam, nor is the syllogism the *only* tool of analysis to use in an examination answer. As described in other chapters of this book, excellent students, as well as excellent lawyers, reason by

Estoppel is a legal theory you will learn about. Under that theory, a person is barred ("estopped") from asserting or denying a fact because of her prior words or acts that were inconsistent with such an assertion or denial. To invoke that theory against an adversary, one must usually demonstrate that one justifiably *relied*, to her detriment, on the inconsistent representation of the other party.

analogy, by distinguishing cases, and by many other means. This preview of law exam answering, however, should give you an idea of what to anticipate, and why continual practice and development throughout the fourteen weeks of your fall semester are critical.

The Analysis

The analysis is comprised of the facts and the law interwoven with the policy, in a way that supports a logical conclusion, as mentioned above. But how does one *go about* the analysis? What are the bases a student should cover in this process of analysis?

After thoroughly reading the hypothetical and preparing the outline of your answer (that is, following the first five of the seven mechanical steps noted above), focus on each issue. For each issue:

- Determine what the applicable law is.
- Determine whether judicial interpretations of that law conflict, and if so, how they may be reconciled under the circumstances presented by the hypothetical.
- Demonstrate how the relevant facts relate to this law.
- If any facts are ambiguous as related to this law, address alternative interpretations of those facts, and discuss them.
- Demonstrate, if applicable, how a "policy" may explain or influence a likely outcome. Interweave the policy in your discussion, to clarify the law, or support the outcome.
- Discuss any alternative argument that may exist. If necessary, run through the same steps with regard to the alternative.
- Announce what conclusion the analysis supports.
- Review the answer to find and patch any holes in the logic.

The Presentation

The logical structure of the answer must be evident in your writing. Rambling diatribes, prolix harangues, and muddled effusions—jumbles of laws, facts, feelings, and conclusions—do not score points with professors in law school, or with judges in court. The written presentation must be structurally sound and logically attractive. Your writing should display the logical structure of your thought. Demonstrate this organization through paragraph structure, syntax, and formatting.

Following is a list of do's and don'ts which you may want to refer to as you begin answering hypothetical questions after the first few weeks of law school:

- Use separate paragraphs for each topic (or issue). Link sentences within each paragraph with linking expressions and connective words and phrases ...

Also	Hence	Otherwise
Although	In addition	Similarly
As a result	Moreover	Thus
Finally	Nevertheless	Therefore
For example	On the other hand	

- Add section headings, and use "white space" between sections.
- As for writing style, use primarily short, crisp, declarative sentences, in the active voice, in a subject/verb/object arrangement.
- Demonstrate your fluency in the language of the law, by employing legal vocabulary properly. Briefly quote pertinent rules and definitions, never substituting "your own words" for precise legal definitions.
- Avoid *repeating* facts. Your professor wrote them—your professor does not need to read them in your answer. Instead, *refer* to them.
- Avoid repeating yourself. Note, however, that each answer must be self-contained. Thus, do not refer to material included in an earlier answer because that answer is in a bluebook that has already been (or is yet to be) graded and, thus, unavailable for the professor's reference.
- Never discuss what the professor specifically tells you not to discuss.
- Always discuss precisely what the professor tells you to discuss.
- Never invent facts. Stick with the facts presented in the hypothetical.
- If you make an assumption not directly stated in the facts, explain what you are doing.
- Avoid conclusory terms (examples: it's obvious that; obviously; of course; it goes without saying that; clearly).
- Explain how a policy applies, but avoid writing a jurisprudence thesis.
- As you review your answer, cross off every element noted on your answer outline to make sure you haven't skipped something essential.

> The better examination answer will simply *refer*, for example, to "the airplane crash." The worse answer will include the professor's elegant narrative, "The plane plummeted 5000 feet through the clouds, twisting violently as it was pulled by the earth's gravitational force, to the inevitable collision with Mother Earth."

If you practice composing written answers to hypothetical questions throughout the semester, you should reach a point at which these various elements of mechanics, logic, analysis, and presentation become *automatic*. By the time you sit for your actual final examinations, this "automaticity" should allow you to focus your attention entirely on resolving the complex legal issues presented in the examination questions, without a thought about how to go about constructing the answer itself.

---

[47] Kissam, 437, 438.
[48] *Id.* at 463.
[49] Mary Campbell Gallagher, *Scoring High on Bar Exam Essays* 43–49 (1996).

PART FIVE

**HITTING THE ULTIMATE TARGET:
BAR EXAMINATION PREPARATION
BEGINS ON DAY ONE**

About Bar Exams

The bar examination (more familiarly called the "bar exam" or simply "the bar") is required in all states as a condition of obtaining a license to practice law. Each state conducts its own bar exam twice each year (February and July); the exams vary in content, intensity, duration, and grading from state-to-state. Passage of the bar exam in one state generally does not qualify an attorney to practice law in another state. Although some states allow for "reciprocity," most require all those who want to practice within the state to take a bar exam. "The bar examination," one bar preparation expert writes, "is the single most important examination in a law student's career."[50]

You should keep in mind from the outset of your legal studies that although bar examinations are not "easy" (in some states, sometimes more than half the examinees fail), nevertheless, these tests are designed to test *minimum competence levels* to protect the public from subpar practitioners. If you consider your first day of law school as your first day of study for the bar examination, and if you consistently strive to do your personal best for the next 1000 days, you should have no problem passing any state's bar exam because the essential skills for success in law school are substantially the same essential skills for success on bar examinations. That having been said, preparation for the bar (throughout law school and after graduation) is arduous.

The National Conference of Bar Examiners reports that in February of 2000, only 40 percent of those applicants sitting for the California State Bar Examination passed. In Alabama, the pass rate was 41 percent that February; in New Jersey and New York, the pass rate was 45 percent. *Available at* http://www.ncbex.org/stats/pdf/2000stats.pdf.

The examinations differ from state to state and are often made up of an assortment of components: the state's own essay questions, augmented by somewhat standardized tests produced by a national group known as The National Conference of Bar Examiners.[51] The time-honored essay questions, produced by committees of bar examiners in each state, have served each state well in assessing applicants' abilities to analyze facts, reason logically, and apply principles of law to resolve legal problems. However, as the number of applicants increased nationwide, examiners realized the need to test more broadly and more efficiently. Thus, the multistate tests were born. There are three types of multistate bar examination tests, all referred to by their initials: the MBE, the MEE, and the MPT.

The MBE

The National Conference of Bar Examiners has produced the Multistate Bar Examination (MBE) since 1972. The MBE is used in nearly every jurisdiction in the United States. The test is comprised of 200 multiple-choice items, covering six subjects: Constitutional Law, Contracts, Criminal Law and Procedure, Evidence, Real Property, and Torts. Nearly 64,000 potential attorneys took the MBE in 2000.[52]

The MEE

The National Conference of Bar Examiners has produced the Multistate Essay Examination (MEE) since 1988. The MEE is a three-hour examination consisting of six essay-type questions. This test is given in fifteen states (as of 2003). The MEE is designed to test the same abilities your law school essay exams test, the abilities to:

- Identify legal issues raised by hypotheticals.
- Distinguish relevant from irrelevant material.
- Compose a reasoned, clear, concise, organized analysis of relevant issues.
- Demonstrate an understanding of the relevant legal principles.

The MPT

The National Conference of Bar Examiners also produces the Multistate Performance Test (MPT). This test originated in 1997 and is used in many states. The MPT is designed to test each examinee's ability to employ fundamental lawyering skills in realistic situations, by providing examinees with the opportunity to complete tasks that a novice lawyer should be able to accomplish. Unlike an essay test or a multiple choice test, the MPT does not test examinees' knowledge of particular laws—rather, it tests their ability to *use* laws to produce a lawyerlike product, for example, a will, a lease, or a legal memorandum.

Each State's Own Essay Questions

States test different subjects. Many insist that the examinees demonstrate proficiency in some fields based on *state laws*, rather than just a general knowledge of law. Here are some examples of what different states test[53]:

- The New York Bar Exam includes the six subject matters covered on the Multistate Bar Examination (MBE): Contracts, Constitutional Law, Criminal Law, Evidence, Real Property, and Torts. In addition, the questions may deal with Business Relationships, Conflict of Laws, New York Constitutional Law, Criminal Procedure, Family Law, Remedies, New York and Federal Civil Jurisdiction and Procedure, Professional Responsibility, Trusts, Wills and Estates including Estate Taxation, and the Uniform Commercial Code. More than one subject is tested in a single essay question. Except for questions involving federal law, the New York essay and multiple choice questions are based on the law of New York.
- Connecticut tests on these subjects: Administrative Law, Business Entities, Conflict of Laws, Contracts, Criminal Law and Procedure, Federal and State Constitutional Law, Civil Procedure, Evidence, Professional Responsibility, Property, Torts, Uniform Commercial Code, Trusts, Wills and Estates, and all six MBE subjects.
- Vermont tests all six MBE subjects and Administrative Law, Agency, Bankruptcy, Commercial Paper, Corporations, Equity, Family Law, Legal Ethics, Partnerships, Personal Property, Secured Transactions, Taxation, Trusts, Vermont Practice and Procedure, and Wills.
- California tests all six MBE subjects and Civil Procedure, Corporations, California Community Property, California Professional Responsibility, Remedies, Trusts, and California Wills and Succession.

Most law schools allow no electives during the first year of study. Beginning with the second year, in most schools, students are afforded a wide range of electives. Doesn't it seem important to include in your curriculum the classes you will be tested on? Commercial bar exam preparation courses, essential to help assure your bar exam success, will be able to teach you the fundamentals of many of the courses covered on your state's bar examination; however, expecting to learn the essentials of *several* subjects, while reviewing and relearning the dozen subjects you *did* take in law school, may be expecting too much. Consider your three years of law school as (among other things) bar preparation, and *plan your curriculum accordingly*, soliciting and heeding the advice of your academic advisor, and your law school's Career Services office.

How to Prepare from Day One

Most bar examinations include several parts. The two most heavily weighted are the multiple-choice part and the essay portion. The multiple choice questions (the "MBE") deal with six subjects most students study in their first three semesters of law school, including Torts, Contracts, and Property, all traditional first-year courses. "To succeed on the multistate," Stetson University College of Law Professor Peter Lake advises, "a mastery of Torts, Property, and Contracts is essential."[54] This mastery begins on the first day of law school. The foundation you lay during the first semester forms the underpinning for the rest of your more detailed bar exam preparation. Sustained, systematic bar exam targeted study should begin during your final year of law school. Bar examination preparation expert Jon Strauss, Associate Director of Academic Support at Roger Williams University School of Law, recommends "four to eight hours per week during your last year of law school."[55] Studying for several months preceding graduation alleviates much of the anxiety associated with "cramming" the memorization of hundreds of rules, elements, and definitions into the ten-week period between graduation and the bar examination. But remember this: the *real* preparation for the bar examination—where you learn fluency in the language of the law and practice resolving legal problems through high-level legal analysis—begins the first week of law school. As you begin law school, you have 1000 days until the bar examination, but the practice begins the first day.

> Nearly all law school graduates attend commercial bar preparation courses. Often, these companies provide substantial discounts to students who register with them during their first year of law school.

[50] Jon Strauss, *Straight Talk About the Bar Exam*, The Docket, Fall 2001, at 12, *available at* http://student.rwu.edu/users/docket/91.PDF.

[51] "The National Conference of Bar Examiners was formed in 1931 as a not-for-profit corporation. The mission of the Conference is to work with other institutions to develop, maintain, and apply reasonable and uniform standards of education and character for eligibility for admission to the practice of law, and to assist bar admission authorities by providing standardized examinations of uniform and high quality for the testing of applicants for admission to the practice of law, disseminating relevant information concerning admission standards and practices, conducting educational programs for the members and staffs of such authorities, and providing other services such as character investigations and conducting research." (January 2002), *available at* NCBE website, www.ncbex.org (last visited August 2003).

[52] All statistics in this section, pertaining to state usage of different multistate bar examination products, emanate from *The Bar Examiner*, 6–25 (May 2001).

[53] For a complete listing of what each state requires, along with a description of each state's examination, turn to BarBri Bar Review pages on the Web *available at* http://www.barbri.com.

[54] Peter Lake, *When Fear Knocks: The Myths and Realities of Law School*, 29 Stetson L. Rev. 1015, 1035 (2000).

[55] Jon Strauss, 12.

SUPPLEMENTS

Commercial Study Aids Descriptions

No commercial study aid can take the place of the hard work of studying law. Nor should any commercial study aid take the place of any *part* of that study. Only by continually exercising your mental muscles will you attain the strength and power you will need to perform at your personal best level in law school. The *very best study aids* are those produced by you. Nevertheless, as mentioned elsewhere in this book, some of the books you will find in your law school bookstore have value. Some will provide concise overviews of complicated areas; others offer examples of how the law works; others include questions and answers to provide essential exam-answering practice.

None of the volumes described in this section are intended to replace diligent, efficient study. These books are all written as *supplements* and *references* to assist students in their pursuit of excellence. Do not make the mistake of expecting any of these volumes to assist you in short-cutting the components of assessment-targeted study. Read thoroughly, brief, attend every class and take notes, transform your notes, prepare course summaries and flow-charts, internalize, then answer practice hypotheticals in writing *in each subject*, often.

If you decide to purchase commercial study aids, you should wait until you have attended law school for several weeks—only then will you understand your specific needs. Use the descriptions below to orient yourself to the available products, and then peruse those that seem to offer what *you* need.

These commercial study aids are listed alphabetically—neither their order of presentation nor the summaries of their contents is meant to imply that one is "better" than another. Each student needs to decide which (if any) commercial aid may best supplement her intensive attention to her casebook and her classroom work.

With few exceptions, these listings are specifically directed toward the subject of Torts, for convenience. Nearly every commercial study aid mentioned is part of a comprehensive series, covering all first-year subjects. You may find study aids in your bookstore that are not covered in this section—although most of the major series are included below. Also, be aware that different sales sites (university bookstores, Amazon, Barnes & Noble, for example) sell different editions of the study aids listed in this section. Some of the specific information in this list may relate to an edition other than the one most readily available to you. The

Professor Joyce Savio Herleth, Director of Academic Support at Saint Louis University School of Law, has published a review and critique of many prominent commercial study aids and useful suggestions about how to use them. See *Using Study Aids in Law School* available at http://law.slu.edu/academic_support/ studyaids.html (July 2003).

Never rely on a brief produced by another student or by a commercial publisher as a substitute for your own brief. The process of extracting the essential information from each case is indispensable.

Never rely on a course summary or outline produced by another student or by a commercial publisher as a substitute for your own course summary. The process of writing your own summary is an essential component for your exam-targeted study.

"List Price" provided is the price at one or more actual or virtual bookstores carrying the volume.

Black Letter Law Series
Torts: Black Letter Law Series
West Group (2002), 338p., $26.50

This Torts study aid provides a condensation of the rules and exceptions encountered in a first-year Torts class, and includes a "text correlation chart" so students can find the areas of their casebooks that correlate to the study aid. Contents include: a 74-page "capsule summary," a longer summary of the law, a glossary of key tort-related terms, interspersed objective quiz questions, and two essay questions at the end of the volume. The author's "perspective" section in this Torts book stresses the importance of reading the casebook, briefing cases, reviewing notes and writing a personal course summary ("outline"), using this commercial study aid as just that, an "aid" to the student's preparation of her own summary. The table of cases lists only 35 cases referred to in the text by name—this book is not designed as an explanation of the particular cases students encounter in their casebooks. The Tort volume also includes a computer disk of the Capsule Summary section, which the author suggests students use to assist in building their own course outlines.

Blond's Law Guides Series
Blond's Torts
Sulzburger & Graham (1993), 260p., $9.95 used

Some bookstores still stock this ten-year old "concise black letter law outline," which provides several flow charts, several mnemonics and very succinct case descriptions for more than 400 cases found in many of the Torts casebooks.

CALI: Computer-Assisted Legal Instruction
http://lessons.cali.org/select.asp
Free to subscribing institutions, or purchase the CALI CD-ROM directly from CALI

CALI is an acronym that stands for computer assisted legal instruction. Individual lessons are often sub-topic specific. For example, one lesson identifies the law of the intentional tort of assault, and challenges the student to apply unusual fact situations to that law. Another, entitled

"Battery Basics," explores the intentional tort of battery. That lesson identifies the elements of battery, requires application to some common fact situations, and responds to common misconceptions about the tort. CALI lessons provide substantial test practice opportunities. CALI lists more than 40 different Torts lessons—the site includes hundreds more, covering most standard law school subjects.

Casenote Series
Casenote Legal Briefs: Torts
Aspen (2001), 238p., $29.95

Aspen publishes *Legal Briefs* for many of the major textbooks—five for Torts, for example. The publishers of this series suggest students use their "totally integrated law study system," including the legal briefs, *Casenote Law Outlines*, and the *Casenote Law Chart*, together with the casebook. The editors warn students that the briefs they provide are not intended to replace the casebook: "There is no substitute for the student's own mastery of this important learning and study technique." (Briefing cases is the technique to which they refer.) In addition to briefs, the volume contains "quick reference" rules of law and a short glossary.

CrunchTime Series
CrunchTime on Torts
Emanuel Publishing Corporation (2001), 327p., $18.95

Crunch Time includes 15 flow charts. If you are a visual learner, or need help understanding how a flow chart can streamline the answering process and provide a "roadmap" for a logical resolution to a hypothetical, take a look at this volume. Other distinctive features include a series of "exam tips" specifically referenced to individual torts. The 67 "short-answer" questions (with suggested answers) are "adapted from" the *Law in a Flash* series. Four complete essay questions, all from Harvard Law School's exam bank, include suggested answers (not from Harvard Law School). This study aid also includes a subject summary (about 100 pages) and 30 "Multistate-Bar-Exam style" multiple-choice questions (including answers and explanations), extracted from a companion volume. As the name (*Crunch Time*) implies, this series is designed by the publisher to provide "life-saving help in the final days before exams."

Emanuel Law Outline Series
Torts—Keyed to Prosser/Wade/Schwartz, Tenth Edition
Aspen Law & Business, 590p., $25.95

This Torts volume, like others in the series, is "keyed" to a particular casebook—in this case, the most popular at law schools across the country. You will find nearly every case mentioned in the casebook integrated and discussed within the text of the material (a "correlation chart" relates the outline's pages to the casebook's pages). In addition to the main outline, Emanuel includes a 77-page "capsule summary" high-lighting the black-letter law. The volume features exam tips, alerting you to issues that often resurface in exam questions, and sets of short-answer quizzes (with answers) at the end of each topical chapter. These questions include many of those found in the *Law in a Flash* series and the *Emanuel's First-Year Question and Answer* volume. Additionally, the publishers have included 30 multiple-choice questions ("multistate-style"—similar to the Multistate Bar Exam format) from one of their bar preparation publications.

Emanuel's First Year Questions and Answers
Aspen (1995), 567p., $23.95

This study aid includes more than 1000 short-answer questions covering every major topic in these six courses: Civil Procedure, Contracts, Criminal Law, Criminal Procedure, Property and Torts. Each question is succinctly answered in a separate section. The book is designed for students to "write a mini-essay" answer to each question and then check their answers against those provided. The table of contents for each topical section details how the questions relate to each topic and subtopic allowing for a comprehensive self-testing capability.

Examples and Explanations Series
The Law of Torts: Examples and Explanations
Aspen Law & Business (2000), 556p., $35.95

The author of this volume begins his preface with these words: "This book is based on the common sense premise that students encountering complex legal issues for the first time will appreciate a book that pro-vides clear, straightforward introductions to these issues, together with examples that illustrate how these principles apply in typical cases." This book—unlike the more conventional "outlines" and "summaries"—does just that: provides introductions, examples, and, as the title specifies, explanations. By employing a (high-level) conversational style to explain difficult concepts, and fully integrating the "black letter law," the book provides students with an alternative mode of confronting otherwise dense material. Three supplementary chapters address analytical and strategic aspects of answering Torts exam questions, including how to avoid making "classic mistakes."

Gilbert Law Summaries
Torts

Barbri Group (January 2002), 587p., $22.95

The "text correlation chart" included in the first few pages relates sections of this summary to corresponding sections of seven major casebooks (the most recent casebook edition correlated is a 2001 edition). A 72-page "capsule summary" precedes the 373-page main summary. Several flow charts and illustrative tables are sprinkled throughout the text, as are many examples of how the law interweaves with facts. Hundreds of cases (listed in a table near the end of the book) are cited, and the Restatement (Second) of Torts is referred to throughout. Ten essay-type "exam questions" include sample answers, and the answers to 166 objective "review questions" are fully explained as well. The table of contents and extensive index allow for finding individual topics easily.

High Court Case Summaries Series
West Group High Court Case Summaries—Torts

West Group (2002), 379p., $26.00

This series is keyed to specific casebooks, and adaptable to other casebooks. The concept of this series is to present students with a framework for each topic of the course, through a "perspective" section, followed by a very brief "chapter overview"—then an explanation of each case in a student-brief style, including a visual aid (cartoon), explanation and analysis of the court's opinion, and definitions of some of the more difficult legal terms used in the opinion. Throughout the book, the publisher reminds students to "read the entire casebook and/or other materials to gain a full understanding of all concepts."

Law in a Flash
Torts: Law in a Flash Flashcards
> Emanuel Publishing (1999), Several hundred flash cards, $23.95

These 2½ by 3½-inch flashcards include black letter principles of law and hypotheticals relating to each rule (with answers on the back of the cards). The cards—which cover most topics in the course—may be more or less inclusive than a particular professor's course; therefore, the publisher suggests deleting some and supplementing as necessary to customize the set.

Legal Text Series
Understanding Torts
> Lexis-Nexis (2000), 459p., $30.00

Some readers have referred to this volume (and others in this series) as a "hornbook, lite." The authors explain that they provide "a readable and concise treatise without oversimplifying the rules or the policy considerations," exploring every topic covered in a first-year Torts course. The book contains many footnotes (including more than 800 case references), restatement references and a detailed 22-page index.

Legalines: Torts
> BarBri (2002), 309p., $22.95

This series, keyed to specific textbooks, provides concise case briefs (limited to facts, issue, holding and the court's reasoning) and succinct summaries of black letter law.

Nutshell Series
Torts in a Nutshell
> West Group (September 1999), 513p., $25.50

West's *Nutshell* series offers pocket-sized books (about 5 by 7 inches) featuring concise explanations and reviews of the basic principles of law—presenting an accurate "big picture." As the preface to this edition explains, the *Nutshell* "must be used with caution and with a clear understanding of its limitations." The primary limitation is the absence of many rules, subrules and exceptions "not essential to an understanding of the basic principles." The goal of any *Nutshell* book is to provide a solid structural framework for a comprehensive understanding of an area of law, not to provide a substitute for a casebook or hornbook. The *Nutshell* index and table of contents are detailed enough so that this book may also serve as a topic-by-topic expositive reference book.

The Professor Series
Torts
Emanuel Publishing (2000), 370p., $22.95

A 45-page "capsule summary" precedes 314 pages of an in-depth "main outline." The capsule summary, as with other study aids, is intended by the author to be used for quick review just prior to exams. This volume includes quite a few examples of how the law works—many of the examples are based on actual (cited) cases. However, the author notes, "Frequently ... I have changed the facts to illustrate better the point I was making." The table of contents and index are extensive enough so students may use the book as a "go to" source for an explanation of a topical area, finding it quickly. The book does not include practice questions.

Roadmap Law Course Outlines
Roadmap Series: Torts
Aspen Law & Business (1997), 468p. , $22.95

The author explains that this volume "gives you a clear statement of the basic rules that most courts apply [and] ... explains the reasons that support those rules." The book includes a plethora of examples, hypotheticals, and review questions (with answers) integrated with subject matter throughout the text. At the end you will find a short glossary, as well as a table of cases and an index, making specific subjects easier to find. The 350-page "main outline" is preceded by a 96-page "Capsule Summary" for quicker reference. The "Casebook Correlation" in this edition (1997), which relates its content to the pages covering similar information in the major law school textbooks, correlates only to casebook editions published prior to 1997.

Siegel's Series
Siegel's Torts: Essay and Multiple-Choice Questions and Answers
Emanuel Law Outlines (1998), 224p., $21.95

"The purpose of this book," the publisher explains, "is to help you bridge the gap between memorizing a rule of law and understanding how to use it in the context of an exam." The book contains an overview of the exam-writing process, followed by 25 essay questions and 91 multiple-choice questions. The questions cover most issues raised in Torts courses, and an index at the end of the book leads readers to the questions related to those particular issues. All questions are answered—the multiple-choice answers are explained in detail. Many of the questions in the book are based upon actual (past) California State Bar Examination questions.

Sum and Substance Series
Sum & Substance, Quick Review of Torts
West Group (2000), 208p., $24.00

Exam hints and examples are sprinkled throughout the 150 pages of the summary—preceded by a 47-page bare-bones "capsule" summary. The volume includes 35 multiple-choice questions and six essay questions, all complete with answers. More than 40 significant cases are mentioned in the text—and the casebook correlation table relates the topical discussion to the pertinent areas of seven major casebooks (the latest casebook mentioned in this edition was published in 1997). The author explains, "This work is not designed to replace careful reading and briefing," and the other components of quality study—rather, the book provides a "handy, readable overview" of the subject.

Powerful Study Groups

Lawyers Work in Groups

Jamaal found it amazing that he actually looked forward to these Monday morning meetings. They seemed to set the tone for the entire week—they helped him get in gear, they kept him anchored, they provided a sense of direction. He was surprised when he was first invited to attend the meetings, thinking that only senior lawyers were involved. That came from watching too many reruns of L.A. Lawyer on late-night TV. Here, in the San Francisco office of McMahon, Jefferson & Kowalski, all the lawyers met every Monday morning. Since only two of the lawyers ever appeared in court, absences based on court commitments were rare.

Every meeting began the same way. The nine lawyers, two paralegals, one law clerk, and an administrative assistant engaged in a little post-weekend personal updating as coffee, tea, juice and water was poured and the morning supply of bagels and doughnuts was quickly minimized. After five minutes of socializing, Mark, the administrative assistant, distributed the agenda as everyone sat down at the ancient oak dining table that served as the firm's conference table. The table reminded Jamaal of the smaller version his great-grandma used to serve Thanksgiving dinner on.

Mark had carefully assembled the agenda during the previous week. It included reports on all the "hot" projects and cases the firm was handling, a couple of intra-firm personnel matters, and a presentation by Charlotte Jefferson to acquaint everyone with the new billing software. Each week, one of the partners would "chair" the meeting; this week, Irv Kowalski was in charge.

Jamaal admired the way the meetings proceeded. Somehow, this group managed to address all the firm's business in 45 minutes. Everyone at the meeting was attentive and alert. What was the word? Focus. Yes, this group of twelve professionals was focused. By the end of each Monday morning meeting, everyone was well aware of the progress of the most important of the firm's projects, and all unanswered questions or administrative speed bumps had been delegated to individuals or pairs to resolve and report on at the next meeting.

After work one Friday, Jamaal met his friend Matt at "The Other Side," a gathering place down the street from their Van Ness Avenue offices. Unlike Jamaal, who worked on commercial real estate transac-

tions, Matt was involved in environmental litigation. During law school, they had been roommates for two years and had remained close friends. Matt was slurping down his second Heineken, munching his way through a small plateful of freebie high-cholesterol hors d'oeuvres. Jamaal preferred Perrier and passed on the snacks.

After listening to Jamaal's description of the Monday meetings, Matt offered, "You know, Jamaal, we do something similar at CP," referring to his employer, Collins & Potter, a mid-sized firm handling everything from marital dissolutions to securities fraud cases. "We break into 'teams,' and meet in groups of three or four—mainly to make sure we're all up to date on the changing law that affects each team's specialty."

Matt went on to elaborate—much of their administrative discussions took place by way of electronic note exchanges. But since courts, legislatures, agencies and governmental departments were publishing opinions, laws, endless rule changes, and guidelines day after day, the lawyers at CP knew that keeping on top of their game required a group effort.

"Remember that study group we wound up in during our first semester at school?" Matt asked. "Who was that guy who kept bringing his two-year old?"

"Rudy," Jamaal responded, wagging his head from side to side. "Rudy loved kids."

"Yeah," Matt recalled, "and he loved to talk about them. Between his kid interrupting us and Rudy's stories about some cool thing his older daughter had done that week, we couldn't get anything done." Matt popped another goopy, cheese-covered, deep-fat-fried blob of something into his mouth.

"We weren't any better off when Rudy left the group," Jamaal suggested. "Remember Jo Ellen and her quest for the perfect job?" He waited for Matt to take another gulp of suds before continuing. "Every time we'd start getting down to business, she'd bring up some interview she had planned or tell us about what kind of firm she wanted to work for."

"You know, Jamaal," Matt opined, "if it hadn't been for Claudine, we never would have made it through that first semester. Thank goodness we finally hooked up with someone who knew what she was doing."

Both men had acknowledged to each other—more than once—that Claudine's experience as a paralegal for five years in a Chicago law firm had redounded to their benefit a thousand times over. When she joined their study group mid-way through their first year of law school, she had suggested they treat their weekly sessions as practice for the types of meetings they'd be involved in with partners, associates, staff, and clients for the rest of their careers. "No nonsense. Focus. Stick to the agenda. Socialize later. Adults only. Time is precious. Know your objective." These phrases were Claudine's mantras.

While working for the firm in Chicago, Claudine had learned how attorneys work in groups and how powerfully effective such occasional sessions can be if handled right. "Hey, guys," she had told them five minutes into her first meeting with Matt and Jamaal, "if you want your study group to be of any value, run it like a group of lawyers would run it, not like a group of college kids would run it."

Thinking back on that comment, Matt reminded Jamaal of their reaction, "I wasn't quite sure what we were getting into. Actually, I remember thinking, 'Whom do you think you're talking to? We were 'A' students in college!' Then I listened to what she had to say and realized that we'd been goofing around instead of working. Thank goodness Claudine came into our lives when she did."

Law Students Work in Groups

Practicing law includes working in groups—that should be an integral part of the *practice* of law you are engaging in throughout law school. Unfortunately, too many first-year students dis law school "study groups" as wasteful of time, irrelevant, and often, as a direct path to confusion. This poor reputation emanates from a simple fact: too many law students think of law school as school, and not as an incremental step in the profession. They remember the inefficacy of collegiate study groups and assume that similar results will obtain. However, law students who approach "study groups" as serious meetings of sedulous professionals, efficiently working toward a clear-cut objective, quickly discover the power of working with others.

Well-run study groups provide support, self-confidence, discipline, and feedback. Poorly run, undisciplined study groups waste time, contribute to low self-esteem, deplete motivation, frustrate learning efforts, and convince students that the only valuable way to "learn law" is by individual concentrated study, amplifying pre-existing feelings of isolation.

Ineffective study groups are marked by some or all of these characteristics:

- Absence of an agenda.
- No discernable particular objectives.
- Nothing written down.
- Lack of rules or protocol.
- Liberal starting time.
- Too cozy an environment.

> Whether study groups in law school are essential, or merely helpful, is an open question. Professor Corinne Cooper, of University of Missouri - Kansas City School of Law suggests: "In addition to providing insight, your classmates are a ready-made educational think tank.... How much of this you can tolerate is a function of your stress level and your learning style, but I always encourage my students to spend some time working in groups. Someone should be challenging your thinking besides your professors." Corinne Cooper, *Letter to a Young Law Student*, 35 Tulsa L. J. 275, 279 (2000).

- No recognized leader.
- Failure of some students to contribute anything.
- Attendance by students who are obviously underprepared.
- Topic drift.
- Formation of sub-groups during a meeting.
- Interruptions by outside disturbances.
- Fragmentation of the group during the meeting, with separate discussions going on at the same time.
- Early departures.
- Manifestations of competitive behavior.
- Bickering.
- Domination of conversation by one member with a large ego.
- Quizzing, correcting, and arguing.
- Mismatch in student levels (in terms of academic capability, preparation, anxiety, and/or actual need for the study group).

Understand how a group is helpful

What can a student achieve in a group that the same student cannot accomplish alone? In a group, every student can practice *fluency* in discussing legal issues. Similar to classroom sessions that highlight interaction, superb group study sessions allow students the opportunity to discuss the law in a non-judgmental setting among their peers and to learn from the insights each may bring to the group. Study groups can be energizing, invigorating, and confidence-boosting experiences.

Limit the size of the group

Two people may have a conversation; three or four may have a discussion; five or more have a party. Study groups of five or more tend to be less *efficient* than groups of three or four. One objective is to encourage ample participation by each group member—three or four students can attain this objective most easily.

Select members who are compatible

The "perfect" study group will continue meeting throughout the semester, and even throughout the year. The members will work closely, and often under stress—therefore, they must like each other, respect each other, and complement each other's skills and academic aptitudes.

Agree on ground rules

To keep the discussions "on track" and to avoid "hurt feelings," the members must agree on a set of protocols, conventions by which they all abide. These rules should include, for example:

- A statement about punctuality.
- Decisions about who will act as the facilitator for each meeting and what that role entails.
- Conflict resolution methods (before the conflicts arise).
- A policy on meeting frequency.
- General or specific agreements about meeting environments, refreshments, and meeting duration.
- A policy about recurrent absences or tardiness.

Consider all the negative aspects of study groups mentioned above and think of how simple guidelines could eliminate each of those.

Always use an agenda

Avoid wasting meeting time deciding what should be done during the meeting. Determine the agenda *before* the meeting, via e-mail or after-class discussions, and then stick to the agenda (the group's facilitator bears the responsibility of keeping the group on task).

Agree on a time limit

Meetings should accommodate the schedules of participants—they must start and stop when agreed, due to the tight schedules of most law students. Allowing the study group meeting to wind down slowly, with no specific end point in mind, is irritating to some group members and is inconsistent with a disciplined study approach.

Use the group efficiently and effectively

Delegating outlining responsibilities to individual group members is counterproductive. Group study should never be thought of as a substitute for independent learning activities. Each member should bring as complete an understanding of a given subject to the meeting as possible, without relying on the other participants to make up for personal neglect.

- If the group is meeting to preview a class session, every member should have briefed the cases to be covered in class.
- If the meeting is to review a concept covered in class, each member should have attended the class.
- If the group gathers to enrich their course summaries, each member should bring a completed personal course summary, to which additions can be made.

Use the group to practice for examinations

Note well: Study group exam preparation does not substitute for a student's personal final examination study. You will take your exams alone, not with members of your study group. When the end of the semester rolls around, it is time to disband the group and go it alone.

One of the best uses of a study group is for exam preparation. Strongly consider distributing practice exam questions (different formats at different times—multiple choice, single-issue essays, involved hypotheticals) several days before the group meeting and charging each group member with primary responsibility for preparation of one or more answers. Each neatly written answer can be distributed and discussed by the group, with a view toward "tightening" the response and evaluating the answer for precision, correctness, and writing style. Tactful critiquing and vigorous discussion of the answers will invariably lead to higher levels of thinking and, often, to discovery of unspotted issues. Encourage lawyerly talking out of issues, in precise legal language. This may help confirm what each member knows, sharpen essential skills of cogent articulation, and result in a broader and deeper knowledge base.

Evaluate the efficacy of the group

Set aside particular times (outside of the normal meeting context) to discuss whether the group meetings are achieving the intended objectives with the most efficiency. Improve the effectiveness of the group by periodically engaging in assessment and corrective actions.

Creating Your Study Environment

Studying law begins in law school, and it will continue throughout your career. Law school, Professor Lake explains, is "strongly oriented around creating people who can educate themselves and continue to do so for a lifetime." Thus, he continues, "it becomes more obvious that one of the major goals is not simply to infuse people with reams of rule knowledge, but to inculcate abilities on other dimensions. This means that not only do we want to see you develop good issue-spotting skills, great analytical skills, and the ability to draw solid and defensible conclusions, but we also want you to be able to work with legal change and to be able to teach yourself when no one else is there to help you."[56]

Have you ever admired a judge's chambers or a lawyer's office, thinking, "This sure is conducive to thinking about the law." Practice working in an environment suited to developing and exercising those skills mentioned by Professor Lake, and carry those environmental habits straight through to your bar exam preparation and your professional practice.

Create an environment that suits your study strengths and minimizes frustration and interruptions related to your study weaknesses.

What is it that makes the lawyer's office so appealing? Why do you get the sense that the judge's chambers are so conducive to legal thought? The reason is this: they are usually designed and furnished in a way that is wholly consistent with the objective of the lawyer or judge who designed the office. Design your study space in the same way.

How to Create the Perfect Study Environment

Consider what you will be doing in your law (study) office: sustained reading of deep texts, rigorous cognitive exercises, writing at the highest levels of your capability, and memorization. For this, you need to muster all your organizational powers and not be hampered by interference from what enters your mind through your senses. You need to approach your work with a sense of comfort and to do so in a way that promotes deep, sustained thought.

> "You need the room, you need the door, and you need the determination to shut the door. You need a concrete goal as well."
> King, 157.

Plan proactively to avoid the frustration of not being able to find what you need when you need it. Keep everything you will need handy and easily retrievable. For example:

- *Computer.* Set up your computer and printer so that you have access to the keyboard and the printed page without having to walk to another room (or even without having to cross the room).
- *Writing tools.* Your workspaces must accommodate writing—even though you may do much of your composing on the computer, you will need to handwrite often. Near your computer, make space for writing and keep all the supplies related to writing (paper, pens, highlighters, ink cartridges, stapler, hole puncher) and computer use in a drawer easily accessed from the writing/computer area. As you begin your organizational planning, make a list of all the essential items.

- *Reference materials.* During your study periods, you will need to refer to reference material often. Those materials will include: an English dictionary, a law dictionary, all of your casebooks, all commercial study aids you own ("outlines," hornbooks, and other secondary sources), and handouts related to each course. Design your study environment with sufficient space for these referential tools within easy reach of your production site.
- *Furnishings.* You will need shelving, preferably within reach of your production area. Your desk or table area needs to be large enough to accommodate your computer (and, perhaps, your printer), sufficient writing space (so that you can shift your chair position and write, without having to rearrange your computer position), space for a large textbook or two to remain open on your desk at the same time, and space for your three-ring binder to sit, open, as you study. That's quite a bit of space. The small desk you had in your college dormitory room probably wasn't as large as the desk in most law offices, was it? Your chair should be the proper height and configuration to allow for hours of sustained use, without inducing fatigue or muscle problems. Find a sturdy office chair that ergonomically suits your individual needs. If cash is a consideration, look for used furniture stores that carry what you need. As you accumulate practice exams, syllabi, study guides, photocopied law review articles, administrivia related to your school and your career path, you will need a place to keep it. Obtain a file cabinet right away, and equip it with alphabetized hanging file tabs. Filing strategy is essential to law office management and should be essential to your law (study) office from the get-go.
- *Lighting and acoustics.* Adequate lighting in the room is essential; often a higher intensity desk lamp is helpful to prevent eye strain and fatigue. If you prefer to work in silence, do what you are able to soundproof your work area. Soundproofing is usually much easier in a true office environment than in a home (house or apartment)—therefore, be prepared to mask unwanted sounds in other ways. Some prefer "white noise" sounds—you can purchase compact discs loaded with soothing sounds of rivers, streams, surf, tropical birds, and waterfalls. A great set of headphones to attach to your music source will often isolate you from

Don't forget an eraser. You will go through many erasers in law school.

Garage sales, want ads, and Internet sources provide a large inventory of furniture from which to choose.

On distractions while attempting to learn, novelist Stephen King writes, "You learn best by reading and writing a lot, and the most valuable lessons of all are the ones you teach yourself. These lessons almost always occur with the study door closed." King, 236.

all outside sounds. Whether you listen to classical music or something with more verve, it should not be music that engages your intellect; the texts you are reading or writing require all your attention. The telephone in your law (study) office should not ring—most of the time, your answering machine should act as your "receptionist," so you won't be distracted from your work. Check for messages during your breaks.

- *Atmosphere*. The "climate" in your office should be as conducive to intensive study as is possible. Adequate heating, air conditioning, and ventilation is essential.

- *Distractions*. Remove distractions from your line of sight. If you intend to read at your desk some of the time and in a more comfortable "easy chair" in your office at other times, sit in those chairs to see what you will be looking at as you look up from the pages. Many are easily distracted by the calendar on the wall, the photos of family and friends, or simply by the design on the wallpaper or the color of the wall. Prepare your space so that distractions will be minimal to nil.

- *Appetite*. Although it's probably not a great idea to keep a refrigerator near your desk, you should plan on having energy producing munchies, as well as water and other fluids, at hand during every extended study period, to avoid those trips to the kitchen that lead to other distractions.

> "If possible," Stephen King explains, "there should be no telephone in your writing room, certainly no TV or videogames for you to fool around with. If there's a window, draw the curtains or pull down the shades unless it looks out at a blank wall. For any writer, but for the beginning writer in particular, it's wise to eliminate any possible distraction." King, 156.

---

[56] Peter Lake, *When Fear Knocks: The Myths and Realities of Law School*, 29 Stetson L. Rev. 1015, 1024 (Spring 2000).

Creating a Subject-Specific Wall Chart

The Subject-Specific Wall Chart is an interactive graphic organizer. The concept is simple—construction of a single-subject all-inclusive schematic flow chart, designed to promote rapid development of the "categories and consequences" thought processes essential to legal analysis. You create it, you configure it, you use it physically and actively. Developing and using a large flow chart for each subject will allow you to interactively employ several "modes" of learning: kinesthetic, tactile, and visual.

Kinesthetic learners learn better by writing information, by using their hands to explain, by practicing, doing and moving—becoming physically involved in problem resolving. Tactile learners learn better by touching and manipulating the information. Visual learners need to "see" information and the organizational, structural, schematic relationships between blocks of information. For all three learning styles, some degree of "interactivity" is of paramount importance.

Construction of a Subject-Specific Wall Chart

Locate a suitable wall in your study area. Although any size will work, the bigger the better—fifteen linear feet would be fine for Torts or Contracts. Using 3 by 5-inch note cards, halved, fastened to the wall with push pins, and connected by string or yarn, construct a large scale flow chart covering all the issues you have studied in one subject. Using the method described in Part Two (see "Fifth Component: Prepare Flow Charts"), construct your flow chart on the wall.

Alter, augment, and adjust your wall chart as often as necessary throughout the semester.

> Your wall needs to be "soft" enough to accept pushpins—drywall or wood walls are just fine. The author's wall is covered with a burlap-like fabric that adheres to the wall with wallpaper paste—this masks the pinholes left by the pushpins.

Using Your Subject-Specific Wall Chart As a Strategic Exam-Preparation Device

Most professors expect first year students to demonstrate their ability to recognize legal issues that arise when parties, circumstances, and conditions interact to create problems, then to cogently explain how legal principles apply to resolve the conflicts. Isn't that what *lawyers* do?

This endeavor requires, at least:

- The capability to recognize covert legal issues.
- Skill in articulation of applicable principles or rules of law.
- The ability to resolve the problems raised by the narrative, resulting in a comprehensive resolution of the ultimate question.

> Where do you turn for questions during the first twelve weeks of the semester? Sources abound. See Part Two ("Component Seven: Practice Answering Hypotheticals in Writing") for a discussion of where to find these questions.

The Subject-Specific Wall Chart provides visual, kinesthetic, and tactile learners with an effective method to ensure success. Initially, locate questions that will require application and analysis of the topics you have considered in your class. When you have assembled your first set of questions on topics you've covered in class, begin using your Wall Chart.

Step One—Read the question while standing

Identify the topic raised by the question. Another way to put this is "identify the issue" raised by the facts.

Step Two—Walk to the wall, point to the topic card, and ask the key question associated with that topic

The 3 by 2½-inch card shouldn't have the entire "rule" written on it, but rather, the key question that needs to be discussed and answered before logically moving to the next element of the discussion.

> "The rule" is the case law ("precedent"), the applicable statute, a "model code," a "uniform code," a "Restatement" of the common law, or legal tradition. Throughout your first year, you will become very familiar with each of these rule sources.

Step Three—Proceed to the next level (3 by 2½-inch cards) and answer each applicable question

Since many law exams present hypothetical facts which are vague, incomplete in their details, or which fall into "gray areas," you will find that your answers to these issue-resolving questions are not simple "yes" or "no" responses. During this part of the exercise, be wary; develop your skill of recognizing potential merit in each side's (plaintiff's side and defendant's side) alternative position, based upon a different point of view when looking at the same facts. Note that the answers to some of the questions may be stipulated in the fact pattern and do not merit discussion. Look for the questions which reasonable, informed, legal-thinking women and men could answer differently, finding justification in the facts, the applicable rule, or the overarching policy which is supposed to be served by the rule. Talk aloud, and move around the room as you respond to the questions on the 3 by 2½-inch cards.

Step Four—Continue this peripatetic procedure until you have answered all the applicable Wall Chart questions

Short, one-issue hypotheticals are often resolved by stating one rule, and responding to one or two subquestions on the 3 by 2½-inch cards. More complex hypotheticals, of course, demand attention to several topics and require analytical answers to many subinquiries.

Step Five—Sketch an outline of your answer and then write the response in full

Return to your desk and sketch an outline of your answer (either in outline or flow chart format), then write the response in full. Avoid writing sketchy, skimpy answers that do not set forth the rich, full, powerful analysis you were able to construct while standing. Write complete sentences. In the early stages of development use your legal source material for this writing process, weaning yourself gradually as you proceed toward the semester's end. You will discover that your reliance on your course summaries and on commercial resources diminishes rapidly as you repetitively respond to similar inquiries.

Step Six—Critique your response

Edit for concision, clarity, fluency and flow. If necessary, check your rule and definition statements for accuracy. Rewrite any portions that are incorrect.

By the end of the semester, in each class, you will have acquired a total mastery of logical analysis of every issue raised by your professor during the course. You will have adeptly answered scores of hypothetical questions, self-testing your ability to recognize issues lurking behind and between facts. You will have developed a systematic pattern of analysis of garden-variety issues and struggled through analyses of more recondite, murky interplays of law and fuzzy facts. In short, you will be ready to perform at your personal best level on your final exam because you have been practicing law for months.

> Peripatetic is an excellent word to use for this activity. It means, "walking about or from place to place." The word, Greek in origin, is often used in an Aristotelian context—relating to the philosophy or teaching methods of Aristotle, who conducted discussions while walking about in the Lyceum of ancient Athens.

Tips from the Pros

In the spring of 2003, I asked law school academic support professionals from around the country to provide helpful tips for law students. I have selected a number of those suggestions and commented upon them. As you read, keep in mind that none of the contributors had read the text of this book—these are all tips that they pass along to their own students. I have categorized the tips to correspond to the Law CATS and other segments of this book.

Reading and Briefing

"No one briefs second semester." Have you seen these words on flyers or heard them from fellow students? The truth is that the best students brief nearly all the cases, not only first year, but throughout law school. Briefing is essential for a number of reasons:

1. It is preparation for writing the final exam.
2. It is the beginning of your study outline.
3. It is what lawyers do all the time.

Analyzing your cases by reading about them in a commercial study aid or someone else's case brief is like trying to learn how to ride a bicycle by watching someone else. When you are in practice, there will not be anyone to tell you what a case means; *you* will be the one telling your client, opposing counsel, the court, and the jury what the cases mean.

Contributed by Daniel J. Wilson
Assistant Director Academic Achievement Program
University of Denver College of Law

> Don't be fooled by those who insist that briefing is only for beginners. Dan Wilson is absolutely correct when he explains that lawyers brief all the time. If you want to become a lawyer, if you want to succeed in law school, do what lawyers do.

Students normally think of their study strategy in discrete steps, such as case briefing, course outlining, and exam preparation. Students, however, benefit from seeing how these steps are related and by combining steps when possible. For instance, when students brief cases, they often move from one case to the next and never think about how the cases relate to one another. They forget that case briefing is like crafting a puzzle piece

> "Where does it fit?" This is a question you should continually ask. How does this fact help or hurt my argument? Why is this case important to me? Lawyers continually work with "puzzle pieces." Professor Gantt's tip leads to greater understanding of "the big picture" and how all the pieces fit.

that, in turn, must be fit together to form the larger picture of the course. To be a good "piece," the brief must have prongs that can be fitted together with other briefs. To develop those prongs, students should therefore include in their brief a section at the top identifying the major course concept and subconcept (if applicable) to which that case applies. Even more important, they should include a "Connections" section at the end of their brief identifying how the case relates to other cases they have read. (Does this case announce a general rule? Does it discuss a particular element of a rule announced in another case? Does it extend a rule announced in another case? Does this case develop an exception to a rule announced in another case?) Attempting to make these connections as students read is important because they know the cases well right after reading them and because this process saves them time later when they try to compare and contrast cases in forming their course outline.

Contributed by L.O. Natt Gantt, II
Assistant Professor and Director of Academic Success
Regent University School of Law

Attending Class and Note-Taking

> Marcia Goldsmith's advice should lead you to wonder, "Why would I *ever* miss a class?" Use of class time to "ferret out clues" is consistent with the objective of targeting your law school study regimen toward scoring your personal best on every exam. Listen to what the person who will be writing the exam question—and who will be grading your written response—says in class. Your professor is your best source for input in the *Language of the Law*.

I am not going to give you tips on color-coding your notes (although that is a good idea) or discuss handwriting vs. laptop (although that is a good discussion); instead I am going to share with you a way to use the class time to gather clues on what the final exam might look like.

Use your class time to discover your professor's likes and dislikes. Does every discussion end with a policy discussion? Then know your policy. Does he/she write hypotheticals on the board or spend a long time talking about them? Then copy those hypotheticals verbatim. Does he/she use the same buzzwords over and over again? Then write those words down. Does your professor spend a lot of time discussing one particular concept? Then make sure you star that portion of your notes. The way your professor deals with hypotheticals, discusses concepts and uses buzzwords are all clues as to what he/she wants to see on a final exam. By using that class time to ferret out clues, you will be one step closer to writing an excellent exam.

Contributed by Marcia Goldsmith, Esq.
Student Advising Coordinator
Washington University in St. Louis, School of Law

You should review your notes every day, if you aren't reorganizing them on your laptop computer. If you don't do this within twenty-four hours, you will forget as much as 80 percent of the material, and you won't be able to remember it when you try to make an outline. Moreover, daily review of your notes—all your notes, from the beginning of the class—helps you to put the material you learn into context within the structure of the class. It also helps you see where each class fits into the big picture. How does Contracts relate to Torts, and what different purposes do those areas of law serve? Eventually, you will become more comfortable with the overall structure of the law. Moreover, by reviewing your notes, you should be able to better remember the rules and the case examples and hypothetical questions that helped explain and explore the rules.

> ...and what better way to "review" your notes than to "transform" them as you will find described as the third Component of Assessment-Targeted Study.

Contributed by Mario W. Mainero
Director, Academic Success Program
Whittier Law School

Attend class and participate. Do not miss class because you are behind in your reading—this will only make you more behind in your studies. Do not miss class because you feel like you know the material already—you are missing an opportunity to engage in a dialogue with the professor about the material and test your knowledge of it.

Law classes are markedly different from college classes. Learn to appreciate the positive aspects of the Socratic Method. While many people find the Socratic Method of teaching intimidating and even alienating, if done properly, it does challenge students and creates an engaging classroom. Keep a good humor about yourself if you've been "grilled" in class. Overcome fear of being called on by volunteering or talking to your professor after class.

> When Professor Todd suggests that you not miss class because you "feel like you know the material already," he's striking at a fundamental issue. You *should* feel like you know the material before *every* class. Ideally, you don't go to class primarily to learn "material." Rather, you attend class to engage in colloquy with the professor and your colleagues.

Contributed by Adam G. Todd
Assistant Professor of Legal Writing & Director of Academic Support
Salmon P. Chase College of Law
Northern Kentucky University

Preparing Course Summaries

Herbert Ramy uses the term "outline" for what this book refers to as a "course summary." He encourages students to build the summary on a weekly basis. What a solid foundation you will have for the next week of a class if you have completed the part of your course summary covering the previous week's topic.

Outlining is a journey, not a destination. Outlining is a process that should begin fairly early in the semester and one that should continue until the end of the year. Classes in law school tend to build upon each other. Therefore, a thorough understanding of topics raised early during the first few weeks of the semester is essential if one is to understand concepts covered later in the year. Creating your outline on a rolling basis can help. For example, reviewing and outlining a week's worth of class notes over the weekend forces you to reconsider that week's topics. In order to create the outline, you will be forced to consider how various topics fit together, and you may even need to engage in additional research regarding certain ideas. By the end of the weekend, you should have a thorough understanding of the prior week's material. Because the next week's class material will likely build on the prior week's topics, you will be in a much better position to comprehend the new material on a much deeper level. In fact, as the year progresses, you may even be able to anticipate the focus for next week's classes based on what you have already covered.

Contributed by Herbert N. Ramy, Director
Academic Support Program
Suffolk University Law School

Practicing Writing Answers

Can you imagine any other performance-judged profession where the person being judged would consider *not* practicing for the event? Can you imagine being on the operating table and hearing your doctor say, "Ah, heart surgery—I've always been interested in this. Why, I stayed up all night reading about it. Let's get started!"

Writing a law school examination answer is a skill that can be learned. In addition to knowing the components and structure of a good answer, you need to practice. As a first-semester law student, actually take pen to paper and write out practice exam answers. Bring them to your professors for feedback. Incorporate their suggestions into more practice exam answers. Do this with each of your professors to learn what he or she expects on a real exam. The first time you write a law school exam should not be the first time you write a law school exam.

Contributed by Carole A. Wastog
Director, Academic Support Services
Louis D. Brandeis School of Law
University of Louisville

Virtually every class has practice exams that are available to you on reserve in the library. Taking a practice exam under exam conditions is the best way to prepare for an exam. What do I mean by taking practice exams under exam conditions? I mean:

> (1) take them in the time allotted, while doing nothing else. If you do not take them as an actual run-through, your mind and your body will not become used to taking law school exams, and you are more likely to freeze up or perform at a less than peak performance; and

> (2) take them when you are prepared, such as in the last two or three weeks of the semester. Earlier than that, you will not have had enough material to be able to satisfactorily complete the exam.

Contributed by Mario W. Mainero
Director, Academic Success Program
Whittier Law School

> Waiting until the last three weeks of the semester is an excellent idea for the exams that cover the entire course. However, you should be working through issue-specific hypotheticals—in writing—throughout the semester. Notice Mario Mainero's suggestion that your *body* needs to "become used to taking ... exams." Physical readiness is an important element of preparedness.

Exam Preparation and Answering

Study groups can be very effective in preparing for examinations, but do not fall into the trap of using the study group as a means of spreading around work that each student must complete on his or her own, such as creating outlines. Instead, use the members of your study group as a sounding board for problems or questions about specific aspects of the class. With more individuals considering an issue, it is more likely to receive a thorough review.

As for exam preparation, try the following. As a group, agree on a sample examination to review. Then, have each person write a sample answer for the examination. Once completed, review the answer on your own and come up with a list of issues with which you had difficulty. Then, meet again with your study group and discuss the various issues everyone has raised.

Contributed by Herbert N. Ramy, Director
Academic Support Program
Suffolk University Law School

> Heed Herbert Ramy's advice about divvying up work. *Never* let another law student prepare part of your course summary or brief a case for you. The learning is in the doing. Group discussion *after* individual struggle can be very powerful.

An invisible being known only as "Somebody"—as in "Somebody told me" or "Somebody said"—stalks the halls of law schools across the country. He (or she?) once convinced a group of first year students that the school had compelled a student to take a final exam while she was in labor. Indeed, "Somebody" assumes an undeserved nobility during the exam period—students tend to believe this being is all-knowing. He (or she) is not. Heed this: avoid the rumor mill at all cost. Listening to statements beginning with "Somebody said" distracts from the important task at hand (preparing for your finals), eats up masses of time, and too often leaves you feeling underprepared, anxious, or inadequate.

> "Somebody said that the exam has been changed to all multiple choice." "Somebody said that Professor Burke never gives anyone an 'A' on an exam." "Somebody said that all you have to do to pass Professor Brown's course is memorize Gilbert's Outline cover to cover." More often than not, Somebody is wrong. Do not waste your time living up to Somebody's standards.

Contributed by Sherry Weaver, Director
Office of Diversity Services
Washington College of Law
American University

Students come to me with practice exams and exclaim: "We've really cracked this fact application business." "Hmm," I say, "well you correctly identified the issue and stated the relevant rule of law. Then your analysis starts at point A, mentions a few facts at about points F and T, and winds up with a brilliant conclusion." The student responds, "But my conclusion is right and that's what's required, isn't it?" Not really.

When writing your essay answer, it's simply not enough to skip along, expecting the professor to guess at the internal workings of your thought process. From your starting point, each fact should link to the next, discussing how it affects or relates to the scenario. Like a monkey chain, you build and develop each fact as you paint an analytical path through the problem. In legal writing, you simply can't jump from A to F without explaining how each thought (or yellow brick) leads to the next, and so on down the line. Of course, your analysis may wind and curve, and commonly split up into several paths (e.g. on one view … alternatively on the other view…) before finally pulling the strands together for a conclusion. But don't let yourself do an intellectual skip—explicitly demonstrate your analysis, brick by brick, logically addressing each relevant fact along the way.

> A monkey chain is a series of monkeys, clinging to each other by their tails, to form a living chain of bodies to stretch between trees—bridging over rivers. Other members of the monkey pack can use this bridge to cross the river. Is this a myth? The necessity of building chains and bridges of words to logically connect facts and theories in the analytical part of your exam answer is not a myth. It is at the heart of legal analysis.

Contributed by Professor Jacline Evered
Fletcher Jones Foundation Center for Writing, Analysis and Research
Chapman University School of Law

Organization is critical. Methodically and consistently identify the overall issues, rules, subissues and subrules. In your application section for each subissue, use the exact "fact(s)" from the exam that relate to the issue. A good exam answer will allow someone unfamiliar with the question to reconstruct the relevant facts verbatim from your answer. This is counter to undergraduate/graduate writing where concerns about plagiarism or repetition concerns require not copying the exact same word(s). Also, in your application section, make counterarguments if there are applicable facts. However, avoid being a robitron mechanically creating counterarguments when there are no facts. Your professor gets to choose if an issue can be "slam dunked" which means there are facts supporting only one argument. Your professor places some facts as slam dunk issues and other facts that can support arguments and counterarguments under a given issue.

> "Was Joan's bicycle crash an 'intervening superseding' event?" is a header. This signals to the reader that you are about to analyze Joan's crash using standards and criteria related to the legal concepts of intervening and superseding forces, which relate to liability for the tort of negligence.

Cosmetic touches will help all professors follow and understand your analysis. It is critical for a distracted reader. For example: use "headers." A header is a short question that should include legal words of art relating to the issue. Issues that are flagged by headers orient and re-orient your reader about your discussion. Use of bold, underline and or italics are helpful to highlight your headers. In addition, skip every other line and use paragraphs for each part of IRAC including the counterarguments. Make it easy for the professor to read your exam.

Contributed by Laurie Zimet
Director, Academic Support Program
UC Hastings College of the Law

Plan to answer particular issues by using your personal course outlines to develop a flow chart or checklist for answering the major issues presented in the course. You need to have the legal rules at your fingertips, *and* you need to be well-practiced in structuring the discussion of those rules. The truth is, most exam questions can be pre-answered by about 70 percent. That is, you can pre-plan how to hit each issues and sub-issue, and then use the facts to trigger the issues and discuss the issues.

Contributed by Mario W. Mainero
Director, Academic Success Program
Whittier Law School

One problem many students have is developing the analysis portion of an exam answer. In many cases students who do poorly on exams fail to address the facts sufficiently. One way to be sure to address the facts is to use a transition phrase such as, "in this case," or "here" after each statement of a rule or sub-rule. The transition phrase should be followed by a statement of the relevant facts from the exam question. Although there will be times you may choose to not do this for stylistic reasons, if you start with the presumption that each statement of a rule is to be followed with such a transition phrase, it will help you to remember to work the facts into your exam answer.

Contributed by Jill Adams
Associate Professor of Law
Southern Illinois University School of Law

Automaticity is the secret. You should be so "rehearsed" in stating the law and analyzing how facts and law interweave for any issue, that during an examination you can devote your time to the legal artistry of constructing a solid, well-reasoned article relating to the *unique* facts presented in the question.

After you read the call of the question, read the entire essay question carefully. As you are reading the question, you will spot issues. Every time you spot an issue, write a short description, like "battery," or "false imprisonment," or "self-defense," in the right-hand margin. Circle the short description, and draw a line from that short description to the facts supporting the issue, and circle those facts. When you have finished reading the question, you can look down the margin, and have, in chronological order, all the issues presented in the question, along with the facts you will use to decide each issue. This forms your "outline" of an answer since the rest of the "outline" should be a flow chart or plan for each issue that, by pre-planning the answer to each issue, you already have in your head.

Contributed by Mario W. Mainero
Director, Academic Success Program
Whittier Law School

Be aware that not all professors, nor all academic support professionals, are keen on commercial study aids. Even those who suggest them *strongly urge* students to use them with discretion—as guides, as "aids," and as a source for hypothetical questions. *Never* use them as primary study resources.

Using Commercial Study Aids

Commercial study aids are the work of the devil. They are often poorly written, they never present the same viewpoint as your professor will about the topic or the case, and worst of all, they prevent you from developing the very skills that you came to law school to acquire. You will learn lots of law stuff in three or four years; some if it will actually be useful. But the most important thing you are here to learn is how to reason, how to recognize significant facts, how to make persuasive arguments using those facts, how to recognize when facts raise an issue.

Commercial study aids will never teach you that. They will take your money, they will make your bookbag heavier, and they will add to your reading load.

> *Contributed by* Daniel J. Wilson
> Assistant Director, Academic Achievement Program
> University of Denver College of Law

Don't let anyone else do your thinking for you. Not a commercial outline. Not a study group. Not the helpful law review editor you have beers with. Not your uncle the medical malpractice litigation expert. This is a *process* that you must incorporate for yourself. Letting others do the processing for you leaves you vulnerable on exams and in *practice*. Use help from others to *reinforce* what you have already processed. To quote Bob Dylan: "You never understood that it ain't no good, shouldn't let others get their kicks for you."

> *Contributed by* Pavel Wonsowicz
> Assistant Professor
> Director, Center for Academic Success and Enrichment
> University of Nevada, Las Vegas
> William S. Boyd School of Law

Some study aids are beneficial if used correctly. Aids that simply provide you with legal rules or case briefs are of little benefit to helping you grasp the concepts and practice their application. If you use a study guide as a workbook, you will be learning the law and testing your understanding of its application. For example, the Aspen Series of *Examples & Explanations* is a wonderful resource. I have found that the discussion of the law is a very useful component to students when they are struggling to put a course outline together. However, students should take the book one step further. After outlining, it is best to do the examples that pertain to the section you have just covered. This is the best way to test your understanding of the law and its application.

I also suggest that students incorporate some of the examples into their outline so when they review the outline at a later date, they have an application of the legal rule or rules. Students who use these resources as a workbook and supplement to their course work throughout the semester are, in effect, preparing for exams throughout the semester.

Contributed by Kelly Levi
Adjunct Professor
Director of Academic Support & Moot Court Programs
Pace Law School

Time Management and Allocation

> Could Vicki Rainwater say it more pointedly? The *practice* begins now.

Schedule your days as if law school were a job. Spend 8 to 10 hours each day "working"—attend classes, read, create your course summaries. Build routines for yourself so that your precious hours don't slip away. As much as possible, get up and go to bed at the same time each day, eat your meals at regular hours, and reserve a part of the week for rest and relaxation.

Contributed by Vickie Rainwater
Director of Legal Writing and Academic Support
Texas Wesleyan University School of Law

ABOUT THE AUTHOR

Dennis J. Tonsing practiced law from 1974 to 1992 in California. He attended Saint Mary's College of California (B.A., 1969), Southwestern University School of Law (J.D., 1973), and Northern Arizona University (M.A., 1995). He has taught in a wide range of academic settings: high schools, colleges, graduate school, and law schools for more than twelve years.

He presently serves as Dean of Students and Director of the Academic Support Program at Roger Williams University Ralph R. Papitto School of Law in Bristol, Rhode Island.

INDEX

professors, xiii, 6, 9–16, 23, 25, 27, 31, 35, 41–42, 44, 46–49, 51–52,
      57, 61–62, 67–70, 74, 76, 84, 86–87, 91–92, 94, 96–98, 100–
      101, 113, 117, 128–129, 132–134, 136, 165, 172, 175

Rainwater, Vickie, 178
Ramy, Herbert N., 172–173
reading, xiv, 3, 10, 13–14, 24, 27, 30–34, 36–39, 51, 55, 64–65, 67,
      71–72, 86, 93, 109, 117–119, 133, 136, 148, 154, 161, 163,
      169–171, 176–177
   active reading, 24, 38
   SQ3R method, 36–37, 39, 116
rehearsal, 44, 47, 92, 104
Roach, Cathaleen A., 74
Roadmap Law Course Outlines, 153
Robinson, Francis Pleasant, 104

schematics, 69, 75
Schopenhauer, Arthur, 111, 122
Schultz, Peter, 109–110
Shapo, Marshall, 104
Siegel's Series, 154
Socrates, 41, 99, 135
Socratic method, 41–42
speech anxiety, 47–48
SQ3R, 36–37, 39, 104, 116
Strauss, Jon, 144
Stropus, Ruta K., vii, 10, 16, 51, 56, 62
study aids, 15, 62, 66, 95–96, 147, 153, 162, 176–177
study environment, 42, 64, 68, 157, 161–162
study groups, 157, 159
studying, xiv, 10, 21, 23, 26–27, 60, 87, 95, 113, 147
Sum and Substance Series, 154
Supnik, Paul D., 104
syllabi, 14, 66, 117, 162
syllogism, 99, 135
synthesis, 62

Taylor, Charlotte D., vii, 10, 51, 56, 62
teaching, ii, 6, 8, 41, 46, 110, 171
tension (in exam questions), 57
thinking like a lawyer, 12, 101, 134
Thomas, John C., 7
TICRA-FLIPC, 133–135